A CRITICAL INTRODUCTION TO
THE APOCRYPHA

Studies in Theology

Groundwork of The Philosophy of Religion   By Atkinson Lee
The Poetry of the Old Testament   By Theodore H. Robinson
Prophecy and the Prophets in Ancient Israel
                                    By Theodore H. Robinson
A Short Comparative History of Religions
                                    By Theodore H. Robinson
Religious Ideas of the Old Testament
                                    By H. Wheeler Robinson
The History of Israel   By H. Wheeler Robinson
The Doctrine of the Atonement   By J. K. Mozley
An Introduction to the Study of Some Living Religions of the East
                                    By Sydney Cave
Christianity and Some Living Religions of the East
                                    By Sydney Cave
The Christian Estimate of Man   By Sydney Cave
The Doctrine of the Person of Christ   By Sydney Cave
The Theology of the Epistles   By H. A. A. Kennedy
Form Criticism   By E. Basil Redlich
Faith and its Psychology   By W. R. Inge
Christianity According to St. John   By W. F. Howard
Christianity: Its Nature and Truth   By A. S. Peake
Calvinism   By A. Dakin
The Doctrine of the Trinity   By Robert S. Franks
The Text of the Greek Bible   By Sir Frederic Kenyon
The Text and Canon of the New Testament
                          By Alexander Souter and C. S. C. Williams
The Apostolic Age   By G. B. Caird
The Interpretation of the Bible   By James D. Wood
A Critical Introduction to the Old Testament
                                    By G. W. Anderson
An Introduction to Biblical Archaeology
                                    By G. Ernest Wright
A Critical Introduction to the Apocrypha
                                    By L. H. Brockington
The Early Christian Fathers   By F. L. Cross

A CRITICAL INTRODUCTION
TO THE APOCRYPHA

by

L. H. BROCKINGTON, M.A., B.D.

Senior Lecturer in Aramaic
and Syriac in the University
of Oxford

GERALD DUCKWORTH & CO. LTD.
3 Henrietta St. London, W.C.2

Printed in Great Britain by Richard Clay and Company, Ltd,
Bungay, Suffolk

CONTENTS

I.	HISTORICAL SURVEY	1
II.	I ESDRAS	13
III.	II ESDRAS	20
IV.	TOBIT	33
V.	JUDITH	40
VI.	THE ADDITIONS TO THE BOOK OF ESTHER	49
VII.	THE BOOK OF WISDOM	54
VIII.	ECCLESIASTICUS	71
IX.	BARUCH	85
X.	THE LETTER OF JEREMIAH	90
XI.	THE ADDITIONS TO THE BOOK OF DANIEL	93
XII.	THE PRAYER OF MANASSEH	100
XIII.	1 MACCABEES	102
XIV.	2 MACCABEES	112
XV.	THE OLD TESTAMENT IN THE APOCRYPHA	124
XVI.	THE APOCRYPHA IN THE CHURCH	132
XVII.	THE MERIT AND WORTH OF THE APOCRYPHA	149
	BIBLIOGRAPHY	163
	INDEX OF BIBLICAL REFERENCES	165
	GENERAL INDEX	168

FOREWORD

THE English text of the Apocrypha on which this book is based is that of the Revised Standard Version. The titles of the books (with one slight exception), the spelling of proper names and nearly all quotations are taken from it. The preference for this version will be obvious when it is remembered that its publication date (1957) is more than sixty years later than that of the English Revised Version (1894) and that much new material has come into the hands of scholars.

L.H.B.

CHAPTER I

HISTORICAL SURVEY

ONE of the earliest writings among the apocryphal books is probably the Letter of Jeremiah, which may have been written at the end of the fourth century B.C. One of the latest is II Esdras the main part of which was written within a generation of the fall of Jerusalem in A.D. 70, that is to say, at about A.D. 100. This last date leaves out of account the Christian additions to II Esdras, the first two and the last two chapters, which were made considerably later. The additions to Daniel and the Prayer of Manasseh, whose date cannot be determined, may also be later, but apart from these it may be said that the period during which the books were written covers the four centuries from 300 B.C. to A.D. 100. Each century in this period has its distinctive features and landmarks. The third century B.C. saw Palestine as an uneasy buffer state between two much greater powers, Syria under the Seleucids and Egypt under the Ptolemies. The second century was marked by the struggle between Judaism and Hellenism and the first century B.C. saw Pompey's capture of Jerusalem in 63 B.C. and closed with the reign of Herod the Great. The first century A.D. was that in which tension between the Jews and the Romans reached a crisis in the Jewish Revolt of A.D. 66–70.

In general, it was a period during which the idea of a body of sacred literature took final shape in Israel. The position at the outset of the period might be summarized in this way: the Law, i.e. the Pentateuch, had already been fully recognized as embodying the authoritative words and commands of God to his elect people. This had been a more or less direct result of the Exile. The words of the pre-exilic prophets, and of the one or two exilic and post-exilic prophets, were treasured, but in all likelihood were not held to be in any way specially different from other literature except inasmuch as the prophets themselves had commanded respect, and, moreover, as long as some of their prophecies remained unfulfilled they were on that account jealously guarded. It is possible that successors to the prophets, that is, those who held themselves to be like-minded, would feel free to re-interpret or expand their predecessors' words. The Letter of Jeremiah may be an example of such expansion. Further, there were psalms and proverbs and other literature which men loved and which they would chant or rehearse on appropriate occasions. But this literature was undefined and there would be little to distinguish it from other literature except its popularity and intrinsic authority. Writers during these four centuries drew freely upon it all, whether law or prophecy or any other kind; they used its familiar phrases in which to couch their own thoughts and they occasionally appealed to it as having some authoritative significance.

By the end of the period, however, there is an entirely different attitude to the literature. A more or less fixed number of books, happily coinciding (or made to coincide) with the number of letters in the alphabet,[1] were held to be sacred. In the New Testament they are commonly referred to as the scriptures and once as the holy scriptures (Rom. 1: 2). At the end of the first century A.D. the Jewish scholars at Jamnia are known to have discussed a few mar-

---

[1] Josephus, *Contra Apionem*. Loeb Ed. I. 38.

ginal books such as Ecclesiastes and the Song of Songs with a view to establishing them as sacred. Further, literature of several kinds was written during this period; some found its way into the canon of scripture, some into the Apocrypha, while some remained outside the canon as part of the literary legacy of the Jewish people. What follows is an attempt to review the main sequence of historical events and to show what literature was written and to what date it roughly belongs. Since the chief concern here is with the Apocrypha there will be no attempt to make an exhaustive record of the other literature, but simply to give an indication of what there is.

The Third Century b.c.

Alexander the Great had conquered Palestine in 333 b.c. and the empire to which it was then annexed was divided among his generals after his death, the final date of settlement being accepted as 312 b.c. when the Seleucid line was established in Syria. In that same year Ptolemy, governor of Egypt, by his victory at Gaza secured Palestine for his rule. The third century was one of comparative peace for the Jews under Ptolemaic rule. Its beginning was marked, according to tradition, by the high-priesthood of Simon the Just who so lived and ruled that his tenure of office became legendary.[1] The peace was comparative only, for although Palestine remained under Ptolemaic rule for most of the century it was geographically nearer to Syria, whose king envied its possession. In 218 the Syrian king Antiochus did actually wrest it from Egyptian control, but in the next year Ptolemy IV marched out to Raphia, defeated Antiochus and regained Palestine. A summary of the relations between Syria and Egypt as far as they concerned

[1] See Josephus, *Antiquities* XII ii. 5.

Palestine, from the time of Alexander the Great to the
time of Antiochus Epiphanes (175–163), of the battles
fought and of the attempt at alliance by marriage, may be
found in the eleventh chapter of Daniel, couched in veiled
terms as was to become the practice of the apocalyptists.
There is practically nothing known of the internal history
of the Jews during the third century B.C. They may have
been more or less passive spectators of the struggle for possession of their land.

A number of canonical books are thought to have been
written or compiled and given their final form in this century: Jonah, Song of Songs, Ecclesiastes, Esther,[1] Proverbs and Chronicles (with Ezra and Nehemiah). Only one
book in the Apocrypha can be attributed to this century,
namely, Tobit. It is a book that inculcates personal piety
and devotion in characteristic Jewish fashion and belongs
essentially to a period such as this in which men were left
free to follow their ordinary pursuits.[2]

THE SECOND CENTURY B.C.

This century is marked by the struggle against the en-
croachments of Hellenism and the Maccabean Revolt. At
the beginning of the century, in 198, after the battle of
Panium (Banias), Palestine passed to Seleucid rule. This
change of rule, though acceptable, as it seems, to the
majority of Jews, was soon to bring trouble. At the end of
the first quarter of the century Antiochus Epiphanes (175–
163) came to the Seleucid throne. He pursued a policy of
Hellenization more vigorously than his predecessors. To

[1] Esther may be later still.
[2] The literature appears to reflect the fact that the third century was
not a creative period of Jewish life; much of the Biblical material is
merely a compiling and editing of earlier tradition and story. Jonah
alone may claim to break fresh ground.

some Jews this would come as a welcome acceleration of a
process that had already begun. Hellenism had made its
appeal to many Jews, especially among the better educated to whom it would appear to offer a fuller life, both
physically and mentally. But there were many Jews who
would avoid Hellenism at all costs. There was a growing
tension, a tension which probably affected the upper levels
of Jewish society more than the rank and file. It was reflected in the priesthood where there was bitter rivalry,
not unmixed with political ambitions. It was also reflected
in the feud between the two aristocratic families of
Onias and Tobias. This feud is one of the well-known features of this period and offers an example of how deep
seated the tension was. This unstable situation was as so
much dry fuel to the spark of Antiochus' anger at being repulsed from Egypt when the Romans interfered. On his
return from Egypt in high dudgeon he found opportunity
of indulging his anger by an attack on the Jews. Changes
in the high-priesthood gave him an excuse. The Syrian
government had acquiesced in the removal of Onias from
the high-priesthood in favour of the pro-Greek Jason.
Jason in turn was the victim of the scheming of yet another pro-Hellenist, Menelaus, who engineered his own appointment as high priest by Antiochus. While Antiochus
was in Egypt Jason, prompted by a rumour that Antiochus was killed, attacked Menelaus and his supporters.
For this apparent affront to his authority Antiochus dealt
with the Jews in high-handed fashion; he profaned the
temple, set up the worship of Zeus and attempted to destroy everything Jewish in the hope of enforcing Hellenism. This was in 168 B.C. Within four years the Maccabean
brothers and their followers had restored Jewish worship
in the Temple (165). The fighting did not end with the

restoration of worship, but dragged on until some kind of political independence was also won and Jewish leaders were in authority. First came two brothers of Judas Maccabeus, Jonathan (158–142) and Simon (142–135), and then followed the Hasmonean[1] line, beginning with Hyrcanus (135–105).

This century had begun, as had the previous century, if tradition is sound, with the high-priesthood of an outstanding man, also called Simon and also designated the Just. The time was ripe for a re-assessment of the fundamental behaviour and outlook that could be expected from a devout Jew, for not only was true piety stimulated by the example of the High Priest but it was also encouraged by the need to stand firm against the increasing interest shown by some of the nation in Hellenism. Such a book was written in about 180 by Jesus ben Sira. In the fiftieth chapter of his book (Ecclesiasticus) we find a poem in praise of the High Priest Simon. Ben Sira was so absorbed in his Jewish way of life and thinking, that there is not the slightest hint within the book of the menace of apostasy from Judaism through the attraction of other modes of thought, nor a hint of the growing power and attraction of Hellenism. The next book of the Apocrypha to be written in this century, that of Judith, reflects a vastly different situation and is clearly meant to rouse its readers to resistance, even to the last ditch, against a heathen foe. If, as is generally agreed, it be taken as a historical novel, then the most natural time for it to be written would be during the Maccabean struggle and resistance to the persecution of Antiochus Epiphanes. But the Maccabean Revolt brought about also the final fashioning of another type of literature

[1] So named after Hashmon, the great-grandfather of Mattathias, father of Judas and his brothers (Josephus, *Antiquities* XII. vi.1.)

known as Apocalyptic (from the Greek word *apokalupto*, to reveal). Anticipations of this type of literature are to be found in Joel, Isa. 24–27, Ezekiel 38 f., and Zech. 9–14, but Daniel may be regarded as the first complete apocalyptic work.[1] There are a number of well-defined characteristics that distinguish this literature not only from all other kinds but also from its nearest neighbour, the prophetic literature. It is marked by expectation of a catastrophic end to the present age and the ushering in of the rule of God; this is couched in mythological imagery and written from the point of view of a writer in the distant past, the author's identity thus being concealed. There is almost general agreement that the book of Daniel was written, and possibly revised twice, during the three years in which the Temple was desecrated, i.e. 168–165 B.C., in order to stimulate the resistance of the sincere Jews who joined the ranks of the Maccabees. The book of Daniel quickly took its place as one of the fundamental and formative books of the Jewish faith. It was probably the latest book (with the possible exception of Esther) to be added to the canon of scripture and is the only completely apocalyptic work to be found there.

Another apocalyptic work written during the second century B.C., the book of Jubilees, was not included in either the Old Testament or the Apocrypha. The next two centuries saw the birth of several apocalypses, but only one of them, II Esdras, was included in the Apocrypha. The Maccabean Revolt had its historians, the authors of I and II Maccabees, but both of these books were probably written in the first century B.C.

[1] See H. H. Rowley, *The Relevance of Apocalyptic*, 2nd ed. 1947.

THE FIRST CENTURY B.C.

This century is marked by the capture of Jerusalem by
the Romans under Pompey in 63 and by the existence of
Jewish communities living in communal centres in such
places as the Wadi Qumrân and the Wadi Murabba'ât on
the shores of the Dead Sea.[1] The remaining Hasmoneans
continued to rule the country for the first part of the century, Alexander Jannaeus 104–78, Alexandra 78–69 and
finally Hyrcanus II and Aristobulus II 68–63. During this
time the Pharisees, who had come into prominence in the
time of Hyrcanus I, were gradually gaining influence and
power. They were sincerely religious and encouraged personal private devotion, although their desire to honour the
law to its very letter led to excessive zeal at times over un-
important minutiae of behaviour. They stood over against
the official and organized religion of the priests and aristocratic Sadducees. The situation changed with the advent of
Roman rule in Palestine. Pompey took Jerusalem in 63
and from that time the country was ruled either by
Romans or by rulers who held their authority by favour of
the Romans. The first century closed with the long reign
of Herod the Great 37–4 B.C. With the coming of the
Romans the cleavage between the Jewish parties was
strengthened and before the end of the century the more
devout and zealous of the Pharisees had begun to separate
into communities. Two such communities have been long
known to tradition, the Essenes and the Zealots. The Essenes certainly, and the Zealots possibly, lived in separate
communities for mutual convenience and practised a kind

---

[1] The date of their origin and settlement in communities cannot yet
be firmly placed. They may have come to birth during this century or a
little earlier.

of communism. The discoveries in the Judaean desert since 1947 have brought a considerable amount of material to light concerning one such sect or community whose identity is still the subject of debate. These discoveries have shown that between 100 B.C. and A.D. 66 there was a strong community centred near the Wadi Qumrân which runs down to the Dead Sea. The members of the community lived in tents and caves clustered round the building used as a community centre. Many things are still uncertain about this community and about the similar one at Wadi Murabba'ât a little farther south. When did they first settle there? Were they Pharisees, or Essenes, or Zealots, or another similar offshoot of Pharisaism? Why was so much literature found deposited in a limited number of caves? Were they used as libraries or as caches? What is quite clear is that this community had a lively interest in literature and that they not only knew and used the books of the Old Testament but also some of the non-canonical books, since fragments of Tobit and Ecclesiasticus have been found. In addition they also had, or themselves wrote, books relevant to their order such as a 'Manual of Discipline' giving rules for the conduct and behaviour of members, a book of 'Hymns of Thanksgiving' in the style of the book of Psalms and containing many reminiscences of that book, sundry commentaries on books of the Old Testament and a book about the final struggle between the forces of good and evil known as 'The War of the Sons of Light against the Sons of Darkness.'

At the very beginning of the first century B.C. an unknown author wrote the history of the Maccabean wars beginning with the accession of Antiochus in 175 and ending with the death of Simon in 135. This is the book called I Maccabees. Some time after this, possibly a couple of generations later, when the details were less clearly held in memory and when legend was beginning to accrue, another unknown author compiled an abridgment of a history of the revolt by Jason of Cyrene. This history, now lost, was in five volumes and ran from 175 to 160; the abridgment is the book known as II Maccabees. Also to this century belong I Esdras, the book of Wisdom and the additions to the book of Esther. It is a significant fact, and perhaps indicative of the shifting of influence, that of the books written in this century, II Maccabees, I Esdras and Wisdom, with perhaps some parts of the Esther additions, were written in Greek, in all likelihood in Alexandria where the Jewish community was strong and lively. We have now reached a time when there was a fairly large literary output, much of which never came within reach of canonical status. Mention has been made of the non-canonical writings found at Qumrân and to these may be added the documents known as 'Fragments of a Zadokite Work' which were found in the Cairo Genizah, first published in 1910, and now found to have very close affinity with the sectarian documents from Qumrân.[1] Also to this century belong the Sibylline Oracles, the Psalms of Solomon and much of I Enoch.

THE FIRST CENTURY A.D.

This century stands out in Jewish history as that in which the Romans, generous enough as they were in many respects, failed fully to understand the Jewish ethos or to allow for Jewish scruples and thus gradually prepared the way for the revolt that flared up in A.D. 66 and ended with the fall of Jerusalem in 70. The city was almost completely

---

[1] The dating of this material is still under discussion, but the general opinion is that it belongs either to the first century B.C. or to the first century A.D.

destroyed by fire and the Jews deprived of their natural and age-long religious centre.

The literature produced by Jews in this century was both extensive and varied. There were the philosophical works of Philo, produced in Alexandria, and the historical works of Josephus written under the patronage of Vespasian. There were the books of Baruch and II Esdras which came to be included in the Apocrypha, and the apocalyptic works II Enoch, the Assumption of Moses, the Life of Adam and Eve and the Apocalypse of Baruch. It may well be that some of the Dead Sea Scrolls belong to this century rather than to the previous one. The two books which found their way into the Apocrypha, Baruch and II Esdras, belong to the end of the century, the latter being an apocalyptic work. Baruch was probably written a short time after the fall of Jerusalem and II Esdras some thirty years after that event.

The surprising thing here is not that only two books from this century came into the Apocrypha but that any at all did, for there were several factors that would tell against further inclusion into the canon, even into the marginal canon. To begin with, there is no certainty that the apocryphal books ever did receive what we may call 'canonical' recognition in the Jewish Church. Again, even as early as the prologue to Ecclesiasticus there seems to have been a feeling that a terminus had been set to the sacred literature which was spoken of as 'the law, the prophets, and the other books of our fathers'; it could not be very long before the collection came to be regarded as complete. The Incarnation, the birth of the Christian Church and the beginnings of a New Testament would in turn drive the Jews in upon the literature they already held sacred, especially when it became a source of appeal for

B

Christians as well as Jews. Lastly, the fall of Jerusalem in
A.D. 70 would inevitably constitute a terminus. The Jews
looked back on an age that was closed and they treasured
its literature and its memories. From that point onwards
they either lived in the past and dwelt on its glories, or
lived for the future, a distant future, when there might be
full restoration. Scholars, however, were embarking upon
a period of Torah study that was to produce a prolific output of literature of which a large part was a gradual deposit
of the oral accretions to the Torah which had been steadily
mounting in quantity since the Babylonian Exile.

Although the growth of the Christian Church in the first
century hastened the sealing off, as it were, of the Old
Testament scriptures and the agreement to regard just
those books and no others as sacred scripture, there is very
little doubt that it would have taken place at that time
anyhow, because from that time onwards there was a clear
recognition in Judaism that one order had passed and a
new one was beginning, a beginning marked by the codi-
fication of the Mishnah.

In the chapters that follow the books of the Apocrypha
will be dealt with separately in the order in which they
occur in the English text, and then, after a chapter on the
way in which the writers in the Apocrypha treated and
used the Old Testament, there are two final chapters where
an attempt is made to assess the place of the Apocrypha
in the Christian Church and in our own age.

CHAPTER II

I ESDRAS[1]

SUMMARY OF CONTENTS

1: 1–58. The celebration of Passover in the reign of Josiah, his death at Megiddo and the subsequent fall of Jerusalem followed by Exile, thus fulfilling Jeremiah's prophecy (29: 10, cf. 25: 9–12). This is mainly parallel with II Chron. 35: 1 – 36: 21 and is apparently included in I Esdras to provide the setting for the story of Zerubbabel and Ezra and to show that the Exile was an integral part of God's plan.

2: 1–30. The decree of Cyrus and the response made to it by the Jews (comprising Ezra 1: 1–11) followed by an account of the frustration of the work during the reign of Artaxerxes (cf. Ezra 4: 7–24). This is intended to bring the story down to the reign of Darius during which Zerubbabel's leadership was exercised. It is misplaced, both here and in the Book of Ezra; no king named Artaxerxes preceded Darius.

3: 1 – 5: 6. The story of the three guardsmen, or pages, of Darius, the third of whom is identified with Zerubbabel[2] (4: 13). They vie with one another to propose the one thing

[1] I Esdras in the English Apocrypha corresponds to Esdras α in the Septuagint, and to Esdras III in the Vulgate. II Esdras is referred to as Ἐσδρας ὁ προφητης or Ἐσδρας Ἀποκαλυψις in Greek lists of the Apocrypha and is Esdras IV in the Vulgate, except that II Esd. 1 and 2 are separated as Esdras V and chapters 15 and 16 as Esdras VI.

[2] It is almost certain that the words 'that is, Zerubbabel' were inserted in an already existing story by the writer who first made the identification. This writer was probably the compiler of I Esd.

13

that is to be deemed strongest of all things. The first guardsman proposed wine, the second the king and the third in the first instance proposed women, but in a second statement[1] said, 'Truth is great and stronger than all things'. The king invited him to name his reward, whereupon he requested the return of the Temple vessels and permission to build the Temple. (This is the only extant version of the story and is clearly the centre piece of I Esdras in its present form.[2])

5: 7–9: 55. Continue the story of the return of the Jews under Zerubbabel, the restoration of the Temple and the promulgation of the Law by Ezra. (5: 7–73 is based on Ezra 2: 1 – 4 : 5, 24; 6: 1 – 9: 36 on Ezra 5: 1 – 10: 44, and 9: 37–55 on Neh. 7: 73, 8: 1–12.)

It will be clear from the summary of contents that the book of I Esdras is a compilation of material from the canonical books of Chronicles–Ezra–Nehemiah, together with the story of the three guardsmen in the Persian court. The compiler's interest centres in three people—Josiah the king, who celebrated the greatest passover festival that had been known, Zerubbabel the guardsman who became leader of the people and rebuilder of the Temple[3] and Ezra the lawgiver.

[1] Why should the third guardsman make two statements? He probably made only one, that about women, in the original form of the story. The second, more congenial to Jewish thought, was added when the story was adopted for a specifically Jewish environment, probably by the compiler of I Esd.

[2] Several verses may have been written in by the compiler to connect the story with what follows, e.g. 4:43–46, 57–61 (Darius has been made to take the place of Cyrus in 4: 47, cf. Ezra 3: 7 where it is explicitly stated that Cyrus made a decree about the cedar of Lebanon).

[3] Sheshbazzar is mentioned in 2:12 as being entrusted with the Temple vessels by Cyrus, but there is no mention of any part played by him in the rebuilding. Thus some of the problem posed by the story given in Ezra 1–6 falls away.

But the story of all this, or rather the greater part of the story, was already familiar to Jewish readers and had been told by the Chronicler (the assumed author of Chronicles–Ezra–Nehemiah). Why, we may ask, was it retold in this way? The answer usually given runs something like this. The story of the three guardsmen came to the notice of, or into the possession of a Greek-speaking Jew who happened to have a special interest in some of the chief characters in the story of the Jewish Exile and the Return from it, and more particularly in Zerubbabel and Ezra. He identified the third guardsman with Zerubbabel (4: 13), retold the story with this in mind and incorporated it in his own version of the events of the Return from Exile. In the re-telling he brought Ezra into even greater prominence than the Chronicler had done and left Nehemiah completely out of the picture.[1] True, there is in 9: 49 a mention of Attharates, a name which may well be one form of transliteration of the Persian word for governor, Tirshatha. It could therefore refer to Nehemiah, especially since Nehemiah is mentioned by name in the parallel passage in Neh. 8: 9, but the verses are not exactly identical, and it is clear that the compiler of I Esdras had no interest in identifying Attharates further.[2] It seemed right to the author to begin his story with a very brief resumé of the events leading up to the Exile—the closing years of Josiah's reign and the troubled years of his successors. Although he kept fairly close to the text of the Biblical sources from which he drew his material, he was not a slavish copier, and followed neither the Hebrew nor the Greek forms at all rigidly; in several places the text is somewhat shorter (cf., for

[1] An opposite tendency may be seen in ben Sira who finds full praise for Nehemiah (49:13) but makes no mention of Ezra.
[2] For Tirshatha see R.V. of Ezra 2: 63, Neh. 7: 65, 8: 9.

example, 9: 48 and Neh. 8: 8) or slightly different (9: 49 and
Neh. 8: 9) and in at least two places is expanded slightly
(1: 23 f. add a comment on the fulfilment of God's promise
of punishment for the wicked which is not found in II
Chron. 35: 19; 5: 1–6 is also an addition). The non-Biblical
material, the story of the three guardsmen, was doubtless
one of the twice-told tales of the ancient Near East. It has
no specifically Jewish atmosphere, and was probably a tale
of pagan origin which had been taken over into Jewish
tradition. The second statement of the third guardsman
may have been added at this point. The claim that truth is
strongest is much more at home in Jewish thought than
that women are strongest.[1] It cannot be determined
whether the story was already accepted into Jewish tradition when the author of I Esdras found it or whether it
was he who first found it and appropriated it for Jewish
circles. There is one piece of evidence that tells against this
latter suggestion: it is the apparent contradiction between
4: 43–46 and 2: 1–11. It is thought unlikely that the same
author would have ascribed to Darius what he had already
ascribed to Cyrus, namely the return of the Temple vessels
and the authorizing of the rebuilding of the Temple. On
the other hand, ancient authors and editors often per-
petrated glaring examples of duplication, so that this is not
a strong argument.

In the story of the three guardsmen as told in I Esdras it
is Darius who holds prominent position as the contemporary Persian ruler during the restoration, and in con-

---

[1] R. H. Pfeiffer, *History of New Testament Times*, 1949, p. 252, thinks
the story is of Persian origin: 'The exaltation of truth as the mightiest of
all things is typically Persian'. R. Rudolph on the other hand argues for
Greek origin, and thinks that the statement about truth was added before the story was taken over into Jewish circles. *Z.A.W.*, Vol. 61 (N.S.
20), 1945–8.

sequence of this the compiler seems to have deliberately made a further change in the order of events over against that made by the Chronicler. He has put the incident about the walls in Artaxerxes' reign (Ezra 4: 7–24) at a still earlier place in the narrative (2: 16–30) than the Chronicler did. We may conclude therefore that the compiler had access to what he considered to be an important tradition about Zerubbabel, and that at the same time he held the view that the reign of Darius (522–486) was a formative period in the restoration of Israel.[1]

The question has still to be asked: In what language did the compiler use the Biblical sources upon which he was dependent? The Hebrew (and Aramaic) or the Greek text? The book shows some marks of being a direct translation from a Semitic original rather than being a revision of an existing Greek translation. We may tentatively regard it as an attempt, comparable with that of the Septuagint version, to render the Chronicler's story of the Return into Greek for synagogue use in the Diaspora, and probably in Alexandria.[2] If the Septuagint version of Ezra–Nehemiah is another such attempt, though possibly earlier, then we may suppose that they were probably made independently of each other. In those days, however, no version would be entirely independent of any other, for in the nature of

---

[1] The actual date of the story, that is, of its first telling, may however turn on the identification, if it be possible, of Apame in 4: 29 who is called 'the king's concubine, the daughter of the illustrious Bartacus'. Two identifications of Apame have been made: (i) daughter of the Satrap Artabazos III and wife of Ptolemy Lagos (305–283), and (ii) daughter of the Bactrian satrap Spitamenes and wife of Seleucus Nicator (311–281).

[2] This still leaves it an open question what language he found the story of the guardsmen in. L. E. Browne (*Early Judaism*, 1929, p. 29) thinks Aramaic; O. Eissfeldt in the first edition of his *Einleitung in das Alte Testament*, 1934, thought Aramaic, but in the second edition, 1956, Greek.

things ancient writers, editors and translators made far greater use of tradition and memory than we are accustomed to do. The book begins rather abruptly with the statement, 'Josiah kept the passover to his Lord in Jerusalem' and ends with an incomplete phrase, 'and they came together'.[1] It may therefore have been part of a longer work of which we now have no further record.

The date of compilation (and translation, if it be such) cannot be fixed with any accuracy, but there are two pieces of evidence that point to a date in the first century B.C., a time when the Jewish community in Alexandria was the centre of much literary activity. One piece of evidence is the slight reminiscence of Dan. 2: 37 and 2: 22, 23 to be found in I Esdras 4: 10a and 4: 59, 60. The other is the fact that Josephus includes the story of the three guardsmen in his history (*Ant.* XI. iii. 2 f.) and seems to have followed I Esdras rather than Ezra–Nehemiah for his story of the period. His separation of Nehemiah from Ezra is further slight evidence of his dependence on I Esdras.

The existence of I Esdras reveals an interesting phenomenon of Israel's literary activity. Within two centuries, more or less, three attempts had been made to present a record of the events that took place immediately after permission had been given to return from Babylon. The first was written mainly in Hebrew with some Aramaic, namely the books of Ezra and Nehemiah. The Aramaic portions are Ezra 4: 8 – 6: 18, 7: 12–26. Then there were two in Greek: one of these is virtually identical with the Canonical Ezra–Nehemiah (Esdras β in LXX), being the Septuagint version and differing only in so far as any translation

[1] These words are virtually the opening words of Neh. 8: 13.

will slightly alter the original.[1] The other may have been originally in Hebrew or Aramaic, but only a Greek version is extant—Esdras α in the Greek Bible, I Esdras in the English Apocrypha.

[1] Cf. the introduction to the translation of Ecclesiasticus: 'For what was originally expressed in Hebrew does not have exactly the same sense when translated into another language'.

CHAPTER III

II ESDRAS[1]

IN the form in which it is printed in our English Bibles
II Esdras consists of a Jewish Apocalypse (chh. 3–14) set
in a framework of an entirely different kind, of which the
first two chapters are clearly Christian and the last two
(15, 16) either Jewish or Christian. All the early editions of
the book, except the Latin, were written without these
four chapters. It will be convenient, therefore, to deal with
these opening and closing chapters first and then to take
chapters 3–14 as a separate book.

SUMMARY OF CHAPTERS 1 AND 2

After giving a genealogy of Ezra the first chapter goes
on to tell of his commission to convict his people, the
Jewish people, of their continued sin against God from the
time of their desert wanderings and onwards, and then to
announce to them their rejection in favour of a strange
people who have had none of the privileges of the Jews (1:
1–37). In 1: 28 the figures of father, mother and nurse are
used; these three figures are next taken up and used in a
rather different figurative sense—that of the ideal father,
mother and nurse of the Jewish people. The father is in-
voked and told that this other nation coming from the

[1] II Esdras is called Ἐσδρας ὁ Προφητης or Ἐσδρας Ἀποκαλυψις in
Greek lists of the Apocrypha. In the Vulgate chapters 3–14 are called
Esdras IV, chapters 1–2 Esdras V and chapters 15–16 Esdras VI.

east[1] will receive Abraham, Isaac and Jacob, also the twelve prophets, and will be given the kingdom in Jerusalem because the Jews will not repent (1: 38 – 2: 14). The mother is then addressed as though she were the mother of those who are now to become the true Israel and she is promised first place in the resurrection, providing that justice is done, and to this end Isaiah and Jeremiah will be sent to their help (2: 15–24). The nurse is also encouraged with the promise that not one of her charges will perish (2: 25–32). Then Ezra, rejected by his own people, summons 'nations that hear and understand' to participate in the joys of the advent of the saviour (2: 33–41). Ezra is then shown a vision of the saints with the Son of God placing crowns on their heads (2: 42–48). The last sentence of this chapter: 'Then the angel said to me, "Go, tell my people how great and many are the wonders of the Lord God which you have seen"' enables an easy transition to be made to the apocalyptic visions of chapters 3–14.

Chapters 15, 16 are of an entirely different character. They are the words of the Lord put in the mouth of an unnamed prophet exhorting the believers to stand firm against the advent of times of calamity during which the nations will be punished for their sin. Unbelievers will perish, but God will act on behalf of the righteous, releasing them from the oppression of the wicked and bringing them out of Egypt (15: 1–11).[2] Egypt, and the whole world, will be thrown into confusion through famine (12–19) and all the kings will be summoned to receive punishment for what they have done to God's elect (20–27). Hordes from Arabia, and Carmonians[3] shall come in strength and de-

[1] The Christian Church.

[2] Possibly alluding to troubles in Alexandria under Gallienus (A.D. 260–268).

[3] I.e. the people of Kerman on the northern shore of the Persian Gulf.

vastate Assyria (28–33).[1] Then there will be heavenly con-
vulsions and they will bring destruction violently upon
Babylon (34–45). The threat is then turned on Asia, neighbour and mimic of Babylon; disasters will befall her, in-
tensified by the ravages of those who flee from Babylon
(46–63). Chapter 16 opens with a cry of woe to Babylon,
Asia, Egypt and Syria for the calamities to come (1–17).[2]
This is but a beginning, the full blow of famine and war
will destroy utterly and those will be fortunate indeed
who escape because they happen to be safe in hiding
(18–34). The calamities are at the very point of happening,
like a woman whose labour has begun (35–39). There is to
be a time of confusion and no one will live to enjoy the
fruit of his labour (40–50). The sinner cannot hope to
escape his fate; even if he tries to deny his sin, it is to no
purpose; God created all things; he is judge (51–67). The
elect will be tested, they will be forced to eat food sacrificed
to idols, but they will turn out to be pure gold (68–73). The
chapter closes with a word of encouragement to the faithful and of woe to the sinners (74–78).

Chapters 1 and 2 bear no indication of date but are
clearly Christian in origin and link themselves readily with
the rest of II Esdras through their association with Ezra.
Chapters 15 f. were probably Jewish in origin, but like
many another Jewish writing, capable of being absorbed
by the Christian tradition. They may well be as late as the
third century A.D. if the wars described in 15: 28 ff. are

---

[1] This is thought to refer to the conquests of the Sassanidae, especially
the expeditions of Sapor I (242–273) against Valerian (256–258) and
other Roman generals. Verse 30 may refer to his advance through Syria
and regaining of Antioch. The dragons of Arabia (29) would be the
forces of Odenathus and Zenobia who drove him back beyond Euphrates.
33 would refer to the fall of Zenobia at the hands of Aurelian in 272.
(M. Cary, *History of Rome*, 2nd ed. 1954, pp. 723–728).

[2] This section has a similar rhetorical pattern to Amos 3: 1–8.

rightly identified with the campaigns of Sapor (Shapur) I.
The earliest reference to II Esdras that shows acquaintance with any of these additional chapters is in Ambrose
of Milan (d. 397).

SUMMARY OF CHAPTERS 3–14

Seven visions are recorded as being received by Salathiel
who is identified with Ezra.

The first vision, 3: 1 – 5: 19. God's people are in greater
distress than their sins deserve and those by whom they
are punished commit even greater sins; why is this? Because men cannot expect to know the ways of God; they
must endure and wait for the time of the end.

The second vision, 5: 20 – 6: 34. Why does God use a sin-
ful nation to punish his people rather than punishing them
himself? History must take its proper course and is beyond
men's understanding. Why could not all generations have
come into being at the same time so that God's justice
might be shown to all at the same time? As a woman could
not bear ten children at once in her womb so it would not
be possible for all generations to come at the same time.
God made the world and he alone will visit it. There will be
a time of interruption in the natural order when wrongs
will be righted and righteousness and truth prevail.

The third vision, 6: 35 – 9: 25. Why should Israel, the
crown of creation, suffer domination by other descendants
of Adam? The race of men have sinned and the entrance to
the kingdom is narrow. It was of Israel's own accord that
she rejected God's command. There is to be a four hundred
year Messianic age and then the end will come, ushered in
by a seven-day period of judgment. There will be a period
when sinners will be vividly aware of their plight and the
righteous of their blessedness; intercession will then be of

no avail, each will be responsible for himself alone. Few can be saved, the end is near and God will save whom he will.

The fourth vision, 9: 26 – 10: 59. Ezra, worried because Israel is to perish in spite of having received the Law, is shown a vision of a woman in bitter mourning for her son. He rebuked her for her intemperate mourning since Israel's grief for Jerusalem was so much the greater, but she was suddenly transformed into a splendid new city, the new Jerusalem.

The fifth vision, 11: 1 – 12: 51. An eagle comes up from the sea having twelve wings and three heads, one larger than the other two; opposing wings grow, eight in all.[1] The first two wings reign, the second[2] for longer than the first, and then it is declared that none should reign so long again. The other wings reign, and then some of the opposing wings, but the last two are prevented from doing so by the heads, which devour them. The middle head[3] disappears and the right-hand one[4] devours the left one. A lion[5] comes and declares the word of God—the downfall of the fourth beast[6] because of the wickedness of its rule. The vision is then explained to Ezra as the working out of Daniel's vision and the advent of the Messiah.

The sixth vision, 13: 1–58. A man comes up from the sea whose gaze makes all men tremble: but they gather for war on him, so he carves out a mountain for refuge from which he attacks them with fire from his mouth. Then a peaceful crowd gathers to him. Ezra, still worried about

---

[1] The eagle represents Rome, the three heads being probably Vespasian (the largest), Titus and Domitian. The twelve wings are possibly former rulers of Rome and the opposing wings generals in revolt.

[2] Augustus.

[3] Vespasian.

[4] Domitian.

[5] The Messiah, cf. Rev. 5: 5.

[6] cf. Dan. 7: 3.

those already dead yet having lived righteously, asks
about this and is told that the man is the Son of God, the
mountain Zion, the fire the Law and the peaceful crowd is
the northern tribes captured by Shalmanezer and now
returning from their retreat, Arzareth.[1] The man comes
from the sea to symbolize that no one knows when the Son
of God will come.

The seventh vision, 14: 1–48. Ezra is commanded to 'lay
up in his heart' the things he has seen and has been told,
for he is near death and nine and a half of the twelve parts
of the age have already gone. Ezra asks to be inspired to
re-write the Law which had been burned. He is told to take
five scribes and to retire with them for forty days. In that
time he dictates to them ninety-four books, twenty-four
for immediate publication[2] and seventy[3] to be reserved
for the 'wise among your people . . . for in them is the
spring of understanding, the fountain of wisdom, and the
river of knowledge'.

These seven visions constitute a Jewish apocalypse revealed to Salathiel, who is identified in 3: 1 (probably by
an editor[4]) with Ezra. Salathiel is, in fact, another form of
the name Shealtiel, the name of Zerubbabel's father.[5] The
first vision is prefaced by the words: 'In the thirtieth year
after the destruction of our city'. These words ought to
offer some clue as to the date of the book. Superficially the
destruction of the city refers to its fall in 586 B.C., but in
actual fact it must refer to the fall of the city in A.D. 70

[1] A transliterated form of the Hebrew for 'another land', see Dt. 29:
25–28.
[2] I.e. the books of the Old Testament.
[3] The books of the Apocrypha and other extra-canonical books.
[4] The name Ezra is also found in 6: 10, 7: 2, 25, 8: 19, 14: 1, 38.
[5] Ezra 3: 2, 5: 2.

under the Romans to whom the eagle vision applies. If this is so the thirtieth year will give the time of writing as A.D. 100, unless the number is simply an echo of Ezek. 1: 1, being meant not to establish a date but rather to conceal it. The visions all have a common background, the afflictions of the Jews and the apparent injustice of life; problems which reached a peak in the second downfall of Jerusalem. But though they spring from a common background they by no means bring a common and single solution to the problems that are raised. In general the solution is that the present world order will come to an end and a new one will take its place in which God's sovereignty will be established, judgment will be given and the sinners and the righteous, whether they lived in the past or are still alive at the time of the new age, will be punished or rewarded according to their deserts.

This interruption of the present world order so that a new order may be established is one of the essential features of apocalyptic literature. It was to be brought about by the direct intervention of God. It was inevitable that there should be many differing traditions about the nature of the new age, about the manner of its inception, the nature of God's judgment and of his rule, as well as its duration. The variety of tradition about these questions has resulted in noticeable differences between the teaching of the visions at several points. Many scholars have been led by them to attempt to divide the book into several sections of independent origin. For example, in the second vision there is no mention of a messianic age, but in the third there is to be a four-hundred year rule of a messianic prince (7: 28). The sixth vision expects there to be a gathering in of the ten tribes from 'another land' to join those who had remained faithful in Palestine. This idea does not occur again in the visions of II Esdras but is found in the Assumption of Moses, 3: 5–14, 10: 8. The seventh vision is unique in its treatment of the revelation of the sacred books to Ezra. The diversity can, however, be adequately accounted for by recognizing that the book embodies, in its several visions, many of the contemporary conceptions of apocalyptic. Rich and varied imagery is one of the recognizable traits. To this we may add yet another feature of apocalyptic writings, that of mystery. The apocalyptic writers were attempting to give a picture of an age that belonged to another world, or rather, two worlds, the world of God and the world of the future. Both worlds were utterly unknown to them and their ideas about them were purely tentative. Also, for many reasons,[1] the apocalyptic writers used pseudonyms and this in turn meant that they thought and wrote in veiled terms, concealing their identity rather than revealing it.

As might be expected with a pseudonymous work, the author has successfully concealed his identity. On the other hand, the time of writing can be roughly fixed. It may be safely assumed that the fall of Jerusalem spoken of is that of A.D. 70 and that the three heads of the eagle vision are Vespasian, Titus and Domitian. Domitian ruled from 81 to 96 and the book was written either towards the end of his reign or very soon after it. This lends some support to the correctness of the date which stands in 3: 1, i.e. the thirtieth year, although one cannot rule out the possibility that it is lifted out of Ezek. 1: 1. The references to Babylon are probably veiled allusions to Rome as in Rev. 14: 8, 16: 19, 17: 5, 18: 10.[2] The author may have lived in

---

[1] See the article 'The Problem of Pseudonymity' by the present writer in *J.T.S.* 1953, pp. 15–22.

[2] Cf. also the image of the lion for Messiah, II Esd. 11: 37, Rev. 5: 5.

C

Rome, but of that there is no evidence. Although the most important ancient version is the Latin one, it is almost certain that it was originally written in Hebrew and then translated into Greek, from which the Latin version was made. It is essentially a book by a Jew for his fellow Jews, to encourage them to look forward to the new age when justice will be done and the righteous will reap their reward.

The Latin version is the basis for modern translations,[1] but translations are also extant in Syriac, Ethiopic, Arabic, Armenian, Sahidic and Georgian, thus indicating the popularity of the book. A notable feature of these Oriental versions, of which some MSS are older than the oldest Latin MS,[2] is that they contain only chapters 3–14. These versions are all probably based on a lost Greek version and were either made before the third century or were made from copies that escaped the addition of chapters 1, 2, 15, 16.

As has already been said, the book is an apocalypse whose author remains completely unknown to us. In the nature of apocalypses, the author is concealed behind a pseudonym, in this case Salathiel in the original work and

---

[1] The oldest Latin MS, Codex Sangermanensis, was for long the basis for all critical work on the text. It has one serious defect—a page is missing which would have contained 7: 36–105. Its loss was discovered in 1856 when Prof. Gildermeister noticed that a leaf had been cut out. These verses are now supplied from another ninth-century MS, Codex Ambianensis, discovered by Bensly in 1875, and are printed in our English Bibles with square-bracketed numbers. It should be noted, however, that a German Bible printed at Berleburg in eight folio volumes between 1726 and 1742 included these verses restored from an Arabic MS in the Bodleian Library, and further, that a German Bible, a reprint of Luther's Bible, printed in Philadelphia in 1743 by Christopher Sauer, included I and II Esdras taken from the Berleburg Bible.

[2] E.g. the sixth-century (Syriac) Ambrosian Bible Codex. In this MS II Esdras immediately follows the Baruch apocalypse and is itself followed by Ezra-Nehemiah.

Ezra in subsequent editing. Neither name can be regarded
as an obvious choice for an apocalyptic pseudonym. A
natural choice would be a national hero of the past who
was well-known to the ordinary Israelite and whose life
was of such a kind that he was very much in God's favour
and might be deemed to have already reached the company of the angelic host. If that were so he would be in all
the better position to reveal the will and purpose of God
to his people still on earth. Salathiel is known only as the
father of Zerubbabel. Ezra is much better known, but is
not a natural figure in the apocalyptic world because of
'his importance as the founder of the Rabbinical line of
development on the basis of Torah, which did not follow
the line of Apocalyptic'.[1] But if it be agreed that the apocalypse is only secondarily ascribed to Ezra, such ascrip-
tion may be due entirely to the inclusion of the Ezra tradition in chapter 14 where the contents of ninety-four books
are made known to him. If it was originally an apocalypse
in the name of Salathiel we must assume that the author
did not go in search of a pseudonym but chose Salathiel
because for some reason it was close at hand. As far as we
know, the name had not been used elsewhere as a pseudonym and had no dead weight of tradition clinging to it. It
may be claimed that apocalyptists never did go in search
of their pseudonyms and that pseudonymity was simply a
trait of their literary method determined by a number of
considerations all centring on a hub like the spokes of a
wheel.

There is another apocalypse, not preserved in the Apocrypha, but found among other apocryphal writings (Pseudepigrapha) which has many similarities and points of
agreement with II Esdras. It is known as II Baruch. The

[1] Travers Herford, *Talmud and Apocrypha*, 1933, p. 180 n.

similarities are striking enough to have raised the question of single authorship, or at least of a common milieu. On the other hand the differences are sufficient to suggest that there were two authors and that the authors may be reflecting two schools of thought. It is difficult to recover the kind of social circumstances in which two such similar apocalypses might have come to birth. They may have been written within religious communities or settlements.

The reader quickly becomes aware of affinity when he finds that both Baruch and Ezra retire for periods of seven days for sanctification, prayer and fasting to prepare themselves for the revelation that is to be made to them. While they are thus set apart the ordinary people are not to come near them. Archangels appear as interpreters of the heavenly secrets; in Baruch Ramiel and in II Esdras Uriel and Jeremiel (another form of Ramiel). In each book there is a reference to special revelation to Abraham when he fell into a deep sleep after passing between the severed sacrificial victim, but the content of the revelation is different; in Baruch it is Paradise, and in Esdras it is the end of the times.

In subject matter the two books have a great deal in common because they both spring out of the same problem, namely, that of the apparent injustice of God's dealings with the world and in particular with the Jews, and why the latter, entrusted with the Law, should be in bondage to people like the Babylonians who are utterly unrighteous. They are concerned to know when there will be an end to these times and the righteous vindicated. Adam is censured as the initial evil doer involving the whole of his race, but Baruch also says that each man is the Adam of his own soul. They address God in the same way, rehearsing his deeds in creation and in the history of his people. There is a strong emphasis on the fact of Israel's election, and on Zion as the mother of her children. When Baruch and Ezra are answered by God or the angel they are told that the ways of God are inscrutable to man, but that they, Baruch and Ezra, must not imagine that they stand alone as men of faith, there are others like them. The world to come was made for the sake of the righteous and the end of time is hastening.

Several sections of each book give a description of the signs that will occur when the end is coming; distress on earth, commotion among peoples, an overthrow of the natural order of things. They both make it clear that any sufferings that the wicked have to endure are their own fault, they had a chance to live rightly and they chose of their own accord to do ill. In both books there is the conception of a specific number ordained by God before the end of the age can come; in Baruch it is a determined number of all mankind, in II Esdras it is the number of the righteous.

After the fall of Jerusalem in A.D. 70, the times were critical and uncertain and it is no wonder that many a Jew was forced to take stock of his faith and to contemplate on the future that awaited him and his people. It was in times of crisis that apocalyptic was born, and here in these two apocalypses we see the Jewish faith asserting itself from two different angles against almost overwhelming odds.

If we are right to regard A.D. 100 as the probable date of writing of II Esdras there still remained a little over thirty years before the Bar Cochbar revolt. Until that revolt and its consequence there was still considerable liaison between the Jews and the Christians and thirty years may have been fully adequate for the book to have found its way into the well-loved literature of both communities. In course of time, as we have seen, the Christians incorporated with it other material that was more specifically Christian and by the end of the fourth century it had reached the form in which we have it in our English Apocrypha.

CHAPTER IV

TOBIT

THE story of Tobit opens with a note of his descent from Asiel of the tribe of Naphtali which was taken captive to Nineveh in the time of Shalmaneser.[1] Tobit then describes himself as a good man who remained faithful to the worship of Yahweh as practised at Jerusalem. He married Anna and has a son Tobias. In Nineveh he not only became prosperous and travelled in the king's service, but continued his loyalty to his religious beliefs and was eventually punished for it by confiscation of his goods and threat of death. On the death of Sennacherib, Esarhaddon[2] appointed Tobit's nephew Ahikar[3] to be keeper of the signet who then rescued Tobit from self-banishment (1: 1–22).

2: 1–14. The family live on in poverty, but one night Tobit is blinded by sparrow's dung after he has performed a further act of mercy. Anna has to earn to keep the family, and Tobit is stung to bitter self-reproach. Chapter 3 describes how two prayers for death reach heaven simultaneously, that of Tobit and that of Sarah, daughter of Raguel, whose seven husbands have been killed by the demon Asmodeus, one after the other. The Archangel Raphael is sent to answer both prayers and to release the two sufferers.

4: 1–19. Tobit recites a number of moral and religious

---

[1] So R.S.V. and R.V. mg. R.V. text has Enemessar.
[2] So R.S.V. and R.V. mg. R.V. text has Sarchedonus.
[3] So R.S.V. R.V. has Achiacharus.

precepts to his son and then (4: 20 – 5: 21) Tobias finds a man to accompany him to Rages where he is to claim money which Tobit left in trust with Gabael. The man, unknown to Tobias, is Raphael. In 5: 16 the story is given an intimate touch with the words: 'and the young man's dog was with them'. On the way Tobias catches a fish which threatens to swallow him and after removing the heart, liver and gall, on Raphael's instructions, they eat the rest of it. The gall will remove film from eyes, and the smoke from the heart and liver when burnt will drive away the demon. Tobias is told that he must marry Sarah and use the heart and liver to drive away the demon, 6: 1–17.

Tobias marries Sarah, drives away the demon, is promised half of Raguel's property and is bound on oath to stay for a fortnight's wedding festival, 7: 1 – 8: 21. Tobias, chafing at the delay, sends Raphael to Rages in Media to recover the money from Gabael and to bring him to the festival, 9: 1–6. Tobit and Anna grow anxious about their son's delay: Tobias is aware that this is likely and hurries home immediately the festival is over, 10: 1–12.

At long last Tobias is on his way home, 'So they went their way, and the dog went along behind them'. The homecoming is enriched by the healing of Tobit's eyes with the gall of the fish, 11: 1–18.

Raphael then reveals his identity and makes a short homily to Tobit and Tobias about deeds of charity and almsgiving, chapter 12. The book is rounded off by a 'prayer of rejoicing', chapter 13, and a final exhortation by Tobit in which he refers to the fall of Jerusalem (586), the Return (538) and Jonah's threat to Nineveh, chapter 14.

Tobit is a delightful story which has the merit of being worth telling both for its own sake and for the sake of the simple religious behaviour and loyalty that lies at the heart of it. It concerns filial piety, mutual trust and love between husband and wife, and respect for the dead. There is a strong faith in God's providence, and although the principal characters are unaware of it until the end, the reader is well aware that God is active on men's behalf and sends his angel Raphael to their aid. These deep moral and religious precepts are blended with simple folklore motifs. It is no wonder that the book has inspired artists and writers and has appealed to men and women of all ages and interests. It has been told and retold. Told originally in Aramaic,[1] if the evidence is rightly interpreted, it was soon put into a Greek dress, and then back again into an Aramaic form that is still extant. At least three early Greek forms were made.[2] 'Is it history?' wrote Luther, 'then it is a holy history. Is it fiction? Then it is a truly beautiful, wholesome and profitable fiction, the performance of a gifted poet.'[3]

Why was it written? Although there are references to the deportation of the northern tribes, the fall of Jerusalem, the Return from Exile and the threat of the prophet Jonah to the city of Nineveh, it cannot be said to be a historical novel, or to have been written to teach history. The human interest is too strong, and at the same time too narrow, for that. Nor is it just a story that was told. As far as we know the Jewish writers of the pre-Christian centuries were not given to writing stories for their own sake.

---

[1] Fragments in Hebrew and Aramaic have been found among the fragments of text in the Qumrân caves. The text of these fragments seems to agree with the longer text of Tobit represented by Codex Sinaiticus and the Old Latin, J. T. Milik, *Ten Years of Discovery in the Wilderness of Judaea*, 1959, p. 31.

[2] One represented by the codices Vaticanus and Alexandrinus, a second by Codex Sinaiticus and a third by MSS 44, 106, 107, 610.

[3] Quoted by D. C. Simpson, in Charles' *Apocrypha etc.*, Vol. I, p. 174.

Life was too grim and earnest for them to develop art for
art's sake. The story was written to embody a number of
precepts and to show that God protected those who lived
by them. Some of the precepts were couched in aphoristic
terms and left to make their own impression on the reader
or hearer, as in chapter 4. Others were dwelt upon and
allowed to be driven home by means of the story that
was woven round them. The two main precepts are
that it is good to give alms, and that the dead should be
honoured.

When and where was it written? This is not an easy
question to answer, and the book offers little direct evidence. It is partly written in the first person as if by Tobit,
who claims to have been transported to Nineveh under
Shalmaneser in 721 B.C. But it shows knowledge of the
Exile of the southern kingdom and of the book of Jonah.
On the other hand there is no allusion to the Maccabean
revolt. The date of writing is thus narrowed down practically to the third century B.C. and there is nothing in the
contents of the book or its literary background that would
tell against such a date. It could have been written at almost any place where Jews were settled and where they
had access to the literature of non-Jewish people. The
natural place to think of is Babylon among those Jews who
had remained there after the Return. The story begins at
Nineveh, passes over to Ecbatana in Media and then returns to Nineveh. In Babylon the author could gain familiarity with non-Jewish ideas such as that of the influence
of demons (Asmodeus[1]) and the work of angels. There also
he may well have heard the story of Ahikar, a story that

---

[1] Asmodeus is a form of the Parsee *Eshem-der* and the Zend *Aeshma-
daeva*. According to the *Avesta* he was the demon of lust. He was one of
the most dangerous of demons.

may have originated in Babylon in the sixth century B.C. and on which the author shows himself dependent (see below). The only serious rival to Babylon as the place of writing the book of Tobit would be Egypt. The main line of argument here is that the fish could be a representation of the crocodile. There need, however, be no attempt to identify the fish with any known species since it is clearly mythological in origin: it threatened to swallow Tobias, and its liver, heart and gall had apotropaic and medicinal qualities. The story of Ahikar was also known in Egypt; fragments were found amongst the papyri of the Jewish settlement at Elephantine.

It is somewhat tantalizing not to be able to determine its place of origin more closely, for it would be useful to establish where in the Diaspora there was a community with wide enough literary interests to have given birth to this charming story. Moreover, as has been indicated at several places above, there is evidence of a fair amount of dependence on other literature. The author seems to have known the story of the grateful dead. The whole book may be said to be built up on the theme of that folk-tale. Briefly the story is of a dead man who, in the form of a spirit, returns to be of help to the man who championed him on earth and honoured him as he lay a dead corpse. It may be found, for example, in the story of 'The Travelling Companion' in the collection of Hans Andersen. The author of Tobit has modified it: Raphael takes the place of the dead man's spirit and the hero has become father and son. Another story known to and used by the author is that of Ahikar. In 1: 21 f. there is a reference to Tobit's nephew Ahikar (Achiacharus in R.V.) who was 'cupbearer, keeper of the signet, and in charge of administration of the accounts' of Esarhaddon. In 14: 10 Tobias is warned against the behaviour of which Ahikar's nephew Nadab[1] was guilty. 'Ahikar gave alms and escaped the deathtrap which Nadab had set for him; but Nadab fell into the trap and perished.' Now the story of Ahikar is, and was, a very familiar story. Not only have we the evidence of the fragments found among the Elephantine papyri, but we have versions of it in several of the languages of the ancient near east and find it included in the *Arabian Night's Entertainments*. Comparison with these other forms of the story shows that the author of Tobit did not limit his dependence to the use of the names Ahikar and Nadab (or Nadan in some versions).[2] He has also followed the technique of interspersing collections of moral maxims in parts of the narrative. For example, at the beginning and end of the Syriac version there are collected aphorisms reminiscent of the collection in Tobit 4. The prayer in Tobit 13 incorporates a number of religious precepts.

When all is said, however, the indebtedness of our author to these other stories is only very small, just about enough to be certain that he knew them both and did not himself invent the ideas. Probably the stories were well enough known in his day for him to need no more than a mere allusion in order to recall the whole story to his readers. Moreover, he himself was too creative a writer to have to lean heavily on other writers, apart from the fact that he had a good story to tell anyhow.

But who was he? This is something we may never be able to answer. He probably lived in or near Babylon in the

---

[1] So R.S.V. R.V. in 11:18 has Nasbas and in 14:10 Aman. The latter form (Cod. A) is probably a deliberate corruption of Adam (Cod. B) which in turn resulted from the dropping of the initial letter. The corruption to Aman was probably made to associate him with the villain of the book of Esther.

[2] Ahikar had no son and brought up his nephew Nadan as his heir.

third century B.C. He was an ardent Jew, steeped in the traditions of his people and eager to maintain the moral and philanthropic ideals of the purest form of Yahwism. One of Tobit's virtues was that he clung to the pure worship at Jerusalem while the other members of his tribe, in common with the rest of the northern tribes, fell away to the worship of the calf Baal. In his treatment of them, the humdrum everyday acts of a religious man become things of beauty and joy and prayer ascends to God to receive prompt and effective answer. We may explain prayer how we will and elaborate all possible theories as to its nature and efficacy but we shall not improve on the single-hearted faith that sees the prayers of Tobit and Sarah come to heaven simultaneously to be answered by the sending of Raphael to bind together both distressed parties in a mission of healing and goodwill.

CHAPTER V

JUDITH

THE book of Judith falls naturally into two parts, the first part (chh. 1–7) is in the form of a historical introduction giving the assumed setting of the story of Judith which then occupies the rest of the book (chh. 8–16).

Nebuchadnezzar, king of the Assyrians, who lived at Nineveh, made war on Arphaxad king of the Medes and summoned the western kingdoms, Damascus, Samaria, Judaea, Egypt and others to his help. They refused, and so when his Median campaigns were successfully ended he turned to the task of punishing the western kingdoms, appointing Holofernes to carry it out (1: 1 – 2: 13). Details of the great size of his army and of the route of the march are then given. As might be expected, they plundered and destroyed as they went and struck fear into the hearts of the people (2: 14–28). In their fear, the people of Tyre and Sidon, and of Azotus and Ascalon submitted to him and suffered the loss of all their sacred shrines so that Nebuchadnezzar alone should be worshipped (3: 1–8). Thus he reached the plain of Esdraelon where he camped (3: 9 f.). The Jews prepared to meet the attack by strengthening the hill tops and laying food in store. The high priest Joakim sent orders from Jerusalem to Bethulia and Betomesthaim to seize the passes into the hills and to close the roads to the south and thus to Jerusalem (4: 1–7). The people all made proper homage and prayer to God (4: 8–15). When Holo-

fernes heard of this he enquired about the Israelites and
was told by Achior, leader of the Ammonites, something of
their early history, and of how, unless they committed a
sin, their God would protect them (5: 1–21). The army,
together with the Moabites and 'men from the sea coast',
took offence at this attempt to intimidate them and
wanted Achior put to death (5: 22–24). Holofernes, in the
name of Nebuchadnezzar (and who is God except Nebuchadnezzar? 6: 2) ordered Achior to be delivered to one of
the cities beside the passes, that he might suffer there when
Holofernes overran the country (6: 1–13). The men of
Bethulia received him (6: 14–21). Holofernes moved in to
attack Bethulia, but, being advised by his officers not to
waste his strength, he set a strong guard on the spring of
water upon which Bethulia was dependent (7:1–18). After
thirty-four days, when the water in the city was practically
exhausted the people of Bethulia, led by Uzziah, decided to
wait another five days and then, if no help came, to surrender (7: 19–32).

The help came in the person of Judith, widow of a rich
man named Manasses, who still, after three years, wore her
widow's dress and remained in mourning. She was both
beautiful and good. She summoned Uzziah and his chief
assistants and berated them for daring to tempt God by
setting a time limit for his deliverance. They excused
themselves as far as they were able and asked her, being a
devout woman, to pray for rain. She then told them that
she had a plan which she would not divulge, but to enable
her to carry it through they must let her leave the city that
night with her maid (8: 1–36). Judith commended her intention to God in prayer and asked forgiveness for the de-
ceit to which she must lower herself in order to bring about
the downfall of the enemy (9: 1–14). She then changed her

clothes and made herself as attractive as she could, to the astonishment of Uzziah and his companions when they let her out of the city. Her sheer beauty, together with the promise to show Holofernes the way to overcome Jewish resistance without loss of life to him, won her access to Holofernes himself (10: 1–23). As Judith begins to tell Holofernes what is her plan she vouches for the truth of Achior's words that the Israelites will be protected if they do not sin, but she goes on to say that they had indeed already committed a sin by eating what had been consecrated to God, and that she was in a position to let Holofernes know when God would punish them. This she would discover in her prayer to him, and for this purpose she was to be allowed to go out into the valley every night accompanied by her maid (11: 1–23). She ate her own food, even when summoned to eat with Holofernes, and she went out to pray and even bathed in the spring of water, the use of which would mean so much to the people of Bethulia. On the fourth day Holofernes held a banquet and was so ravished with Judith's beauty that he indulged more than usual until he was overcome with wine (12: 1–20). Judith seized her opportunity and when she was left alone with him cut off his head and escaped with her maid, under pretext of going to prayer as had been her habit, to the gates of Bethulia. There the joy was boundless when they knew what she had done (13: 1–20). She advised them to hang the head on the city wall and then to be in readiness to take advantage of the confusion that would occur in Holofernes' camp. Achior, when he heard what she had done, was converted and became a Jew. When the Assyrian officers discovered Holofernes' body next morning they panicked (14: 1–19). The Assyrian soldiers also panicked and the Israelites were able to drive home their advantage and

routed the enemy completely. Judith was given great
honour and rewarded with the silver and other goods that
had belonged to Holofernes (15: 1–13). The book closes with
a hymn of thanksgiving and a note that Judith dedicated to
God all that had belonged to Holofernes, and then lived a
long and honoured life (16: 1–25).

This is nothing more than a story told with a purpose.
It is told to encourage adherence to faith in God even in
the direst circumstances, and to stimulate its readers to
show courage in face of adversity. Judith is a supreme example of such courage. Although a woman and a widow,
she put aside all personal considerations for the sake of her
religion and of her people who worshipped God with her.
The story is given a historical setting, consonant, presumably, with the situation out of which it sprang. The setting
is one of overwhelming military attack and oppression, the
latter being as much religious as military because of the
claim made on behalf of the oppressor, Nebuchadnezzar,
that he alone is God and that he is lord of the whole earth.
The period into which the book most easily fits is that of
the Maccabean revolt against the oppression of Antiochus
Epiphanes in the interests of Hellenism. Further evidence
of a second-century date may be seen in the zealous
attitude shown towards observance of the Law and
in the eagerness with which festivals and sabbaths are
kept. This latter is wholly in keeping with the Pharisaic
outlook.

The historical introduction may seem to many a reader
to be unnecessarily long, since it occupies nearly half the
book. Judged by our standards of writing it certainly is
long, but the author may have felt that his didactic purpose would be best served by lending the story the support

D

of a potentially possible, if not altogether true, historical situation. Disappointment is given to the modern reader, however, when he finds that the introduction, long as it is, offers no reliable historical information either regarding the time in which the action is supposed to have taken place, i.e. under Nebuchadnezzar, or of the time in which modern scholars believe the book to have been written, i.e. the second century B.C.

It begins with a reference to Nebuchadnezzar's twelfth year, which would be 593, but the story is couched in terms that preclude any recognition of a first attack on Judaea and a deportation of some of its inhabitants in 597. In 4: 3, however, the time changes to the period shortly after the return from Exile, although Nebuchadnezzar is presumed to be still reigning. No trace can be found of a ruler of the Medes named Arphaxad (1: 1) and the nearest historical point of contact with what is said of him in Judith is the mention by Herodotus of a Deioces who fortified Ecbatana in about 700. Nothing is known of a Holofernes (2: 4) or a Bagoas (12: 11) for the period during which Nebuchadnezzar ruled, but both names occur in records of a campaign against Phoenicia and Egypt by Artaxerxes III (Ochus) about 350 B.C. They are names of generals in Artaxerxes' army. This, then, may be the source of the names and the campaign itself may have been in the author's mind as he wrote.[1] The names also occur in later records and are therefore not safe guides for any accurate data. Joakim (4: 6) is one of the commoner priestly names and offers no help in dating the book or reconstructing the historical background. The king Arioch who is mentioned in 1: 6 is almost certainly taken from Gen. 14: 1. There are

---

[1] Diodorus 31: 19; cf. R. Kittel, *Geschichte des Volkes Israel*, Vol. 3, 1929, p. 677.

other places in the book where the author shows direct dependence on the Old Testament.

It may be held confidently that the whole of the historical section of the book was written by the author as a setting for Judith's achievement and that he borrowed such names and events as suited his purpose from the history that was known to him. He probably drew largely on his own memory, if not entirely so, and made little or no use of written documents. The numbers of the army commanded by Holofernes, given as a hundred and twenty thousand foot soldiers and twelve thousand cavalry,[1] are clearly meant to set Judith's single-handed exploit into greater relief.

If the author is not writing history, what is he doing? The answer is that he is summoning the Israelites to resistance at a time when a foreign ruler, represented in the story by Nebuchadnezzar and his general Holofernes, is oppressing Israel and attempting to displace the national religion in his own interests. Attention is drawn to what even a woman can do when duty and necessity compel. The time of the Maccabean revolt when Antiochus Epiphanes set up the worship of Zeus in the Jewish Temple and forbade the continuation of Jewish worship is the most natural setting in which to place the book.

This date is supported by the pietistic emphasis that appears throughout the book and which is characteristic of the behaviour of the Pharisees who emerged as a distinct and recognizable party in the reign of John Hyrcanus (135–105). The implication, in chapters 2–4, that Galilee and the coastal plain were not incorporated in Judaea, implies a date prior to Alexander Jannaeus (102–76) in whose reign the coastal regions were annexed.

The evidence for the Pharisee-like outlook of the book is

[1] Solomon had twelve thousand cavalry, I Kgs. 10: 26.

this. Judith resorts to God in prayer at any and every time of trouble and before any serious and difficult undertaking (9: 2–14, 11: 17, 12: 6, 13: 4, 7). Her religious life was not limited to what she did when difficulties arose; she was exemplary in her devotion, observing not only the Sabbaths and New moons but also the eves of each of these festival days (8: 5, 6). She fasted regularly on all days except the Sabbaths and New moons and the days preceding them. When she was in the Assyrian camp she still observed such religious practices as she could; she ate only the food she had taken with her, and bathed herself before eating, although in this latter practice there was a deliberate policy paving the way for her escape (8: 5, 6, 12: 2, 8, 9). The ordinary people also observed the strict rules of their religion; they resorted to fasting and self-mortification (4: 9, 12) and were mindful of the fact that God would punish the people for their own sins and for the sins of their fathers. In their pride they felt themselves to be safe from punishment, at least from severe punishment, for they thought their sin was slight indeed. The development of the story, however, demanded from them a breach in their pious pursuit of the terms of the Law. Under duress they reluctantly agreed to use the first fruits and tithes for their own consumption that they might maintain their resistance the longer. They were careful to consult the senate at Jerusalem before committing this breach (11: 13, 14). The author makes it quite clear that this was all wrong and that in consequence God would deliver them up to their enemies. Judith declares this belief to Holofernes: 'our nation cannot be punished, nor can the sword prevail against them, unless they sin against their God' (11: 10).

When it was all over, the Assyrians routed and the spoil brought in, the people worshipped God, purified themselves and made appropriate sacrifices and free-will offerings. Judith dedicated the stuff that had belonged to Holofernes himself and had been given to her, as a votive offering to the Lord (16: 18, 19).

The part played by Achior, the leader of the Ammonites, in the story seems to be that of throwing the religious element into relief. It is through him that the author first voices the belief and principle that Israel can only be beaten if God allows it because of a sin against him (5: 17 ff.). Though an Ammonite, Achior expresses full sympathy with the Israelite faith, and when the battle is over he is converted and circumcized (14: 10).

THE BOOK OF JUDITH AND THE OLD TESTAMENT

In Judith, as indeed in many another book in the Apocrypha, the Old Testament is the major, if not the sole, literary background. It is not mentioned in any way, but simply taken for granted and drawn upon as a very well-known national inheritance. The figure of Judith invites comparison with that of Deborah for the way in which, though a woman, she stood alone to rescue her people from the clutches of the enemy. Her despatch of Holofernes is comparable with Jael's slaughter of Sisera. Judith's achievement, like that of Deborah and Jael, was celebrated in a song of victory (Judith 16: 2–17). It would appear as if the author took Deborah as the model for his Judith. Again, there is a strong reminiscence of Dan. 3 in the claim to divine honours that is made on behalf of Nebuchadnezzar by Holofernes (3: 8). 'Who is God except Nebuchadnezzar?' asked Holofernes (6: 2). The part played by Holofernes in the story seems to be that of standing proxy to Nebuchadnezzar. The latter is the villain of the piece and Holofernes merely represents him.

The reference to the manner in which Judith's husband
died (8: 3) is almost certainly based on the story of the
Shunammite's son in II Kings 4: 18 ff. In many another
passage the Old Testament is quietly drawn upon, whether
it be Achior rehearsing the history of the Jewish people[1]
(5: 5 ff.) or Judith and the people echoing some of the
psalms as they chant their hymn of praise (16: 2–17).

THE LANGUAGE OF THE BOOK

Four different forms of an ancient Greek version of the
book are distinguishable among the manuscripts.[2] This
would suggest that it was a popular book, much used and
copied or re-translated, without being held in such sanctity
as to result in a rigid text form. The oldest known manu-
script is an ostrakon believed to belong to the second half
of the third century A.D. It contains chapter 15: 1–7 and
was recovered in Cairo in 1946. Both the Old Latin and the
Vulgate are based on Greek versions but they show certain
deviations from each and all of the Greek forms and from
each other that suggest alterations in the interests of piety
and morals. Jerome claimed to have used a Semitic version.
Of such a version there is no direct trace, but two things
may be said; first, that the idiom of the Greek versions
shows so many hebraisms as to make it probable that the
book was originally written in Hebrew, and second, there
may have been 'targums' of the book in existence in
Jerome's day, on one of which, perhaps in Aramaic, he
may have been dependent and which may have been the
source of some of the variations in the Vulgate.

[1] Cf. a similar rehearsal of early history in Wisd. 10.
[2] They are represented by (i) the LXX (i.e. ℵ A. B.) etc.; (ii) Codd. 19,
108; (iii) Cod. 58; (iv) Codd. 106, 107.

CHAPTER VI

THE ADDITIONS TO THE BOOK OF ESTHER

OR

THE REST OF THE CHAPTERS OF THE BOOK OF ESTHER[1]

THE canonical book of Esther, which was probably written towards the end of the second century B.C. during the reign of John Hyrcanus (135–105), appears to have been a popular work and widely read. At a very early date it was subjected to revision, several additions of varying length being made to it. One of these additions seems to have been made at an early enough date to have been included in the canonical book, the passage that runs from 9: 20 to 10: 3 (9: 19 makes a fitting conclusion to a book). The purpose of this addition, if it is such, seems to be the recognition and establishment of a change in the practice of celebrating Purim, a change whereby both the 14th and the 15th of Adar became festival days in both town and country.

Further additions were made later and are incorporated in the Greek version of Esther. It is these that constitute the apocryphal chapters. In the Greek Bible the additions are made within the text at appropriate places. Jerome, basing his translation (the Vulgate) on the Hebrew text,

---

[1] The first of these titles is that of the R.S.V. and the second that of the A.V. and R.V.

49

separated these additions and put them at the end of the book where, when chapter and verse numberings were made, they became chapters 10: 4 to 16: 24. Luther separated them more completely and relegated them to the Apocrypha. The English versions follow the numbering of the Vulgate; in R.S.V. they are printed in the order in which they appear in the Greek Bible, i.e. with 10: 4 – 11: 1 at the end, but in A.V. and R.V. the chapters run consecutively 10: 4 to 16: 24.

It will be convenient to set out the additions, by way of summary, in the order in which they occur in the Greek book of Esther. There are six separate additions, represented below by letters.

A. 11: 2 – 12: 6 stands at the head of the Greek book and after giving the date, the second year of Artaxerxes, relates a dream which Mordecai had. In it he saw two dragons coming out of confusion and roaring. The righteous nations cried to God and there came a river and a great light. Mordecai then overheard two Eunuchs planning the king's death; he was rewarded for revealing the plot, but Haman's jealousy was aroused.

Then follows Esther 1: 1 to 3: 13.

B. 13: 1–7. A copy of the letter mentioned in 3: 13 as sent to all the officers of the provinces. It is, in effect, an expansion of 3: 13 and contains a high commendation of Haman, but the date for the massacre of the Jews is given as the 14th of Adar and not the 13th as in 3: 13.

Then follows Esther 3: 14 to 4: 17.

C. 13: 8–18. The prayer made by Mordecai when he is commanded by Esther to gather the Jews in Susa and to fast.

D. 14: 1 – 15: 16. Esther's prayer followed by an account of her entry into the king's presence where she fainted at sight of him. This expands and displaces Esther 5: 1, 2.

Then follows Esther 5: 3 to 8: 12.

E. 16: 1–24. A copy of the king's letter allowing the Jews to retaliate on the 13th of Adar.

Then follows Esther 8: 13 to 10: 3.

F. 10: 4 – 11: 1. Epilogue, spoken by Mordecai, refer- ring to the dream recorded in the first addition (11: 5– 10); the river which became a light was Esther, the two dragons were Mordecai and Haman. A colophon (11: 1) adds that in the fourth year of Ptolemy and Cleopatra this letter about Purim was brought to Egypt, having already been translated.

THE PURPOSE OF THE ADDITIONS

In general it may be said that the additions were by way of revision to make an already acceptable and popular book even more acceptable. Four specific reasons may be noted. First, if it be rightly regarded as an addition, there is 9: 20 – 10: 3 which is clearly intended to harmonize the record with current usage (see above). Second, the prayers of Mordecai and Esther must have been intended not only to complete the story but to strengthen the religious ele- ment in a book which showed practically none in its origi- nal form. The prayers are simple and sincere, reflecting a deep trust in God and calling to mind his mercies to Israel. Third, the addition of what purport to be the exact words of the two royal edicts lends a greater air of trustworthi- ness and historical accuracy. Lastly, the prologue and epilogue (A and F), which set the original story within the framework of a dream vision are probably to be regarded as the work of one who thought not only to strengthen the religious character of the book but also to improve on the story-teller's art.

LANGUAGE AND DATE

The style of B and E and the absence in them of hebraisms is strong evidence in favour of assuming a Greek original for these two sections at least. The rest may also have been written in Greek. There are not enough semitisms in them to demand either a Hebrew or an Aramaic original, and what semitisms there are may be readily explained as springing from the author's native Jewish idiom. It might, however, be possible to argue that they were originally written in Hebrew.[1] The arguments either way are not very strong.

The date of their composition cannot be determined with any more accuracy than the language in which they were written. The evidence, slender though it is, points towards a date in the first century B.C. shortly before[2] or shortly after[3] the translation of the book of Esther into Greek by Lysimachus of Jerusalem. According to the colophon (11: 1) it was translated by Lysimachus and then taken to Egypt in the fourth year of Ptolemy and Cleopatra. This might refer to Ptolemy XII who ruled jointly with Cleopatra V 80–58, 55–51 B.C.[4] The additions were already a part of the book of Esther in the time of Josephus who made use of all but A and F in *Antiquities* XI. vi.

---

[1] As Eissfeldt implies, *Einleitung*[2], pp. 732f.
[2] So Eissfeldt.
[3] So Gregg (in Charles, *Apocrypha etc.*).
[4] But several Ptolemies married a Cleopatra: V, 210–180, VI, 181–145, VIII, 170–116, XIV, 51–44.

THE CO-ORDINATION OF THE ADDITIONS WITH THE CANONICAL BOOK

The additions assume the same historical background as the book and there is no serious divergence of fact between them. The placing of one addition at the head of the book made it necessary to anticipate in 11: 2–4 the details found in 2: 5 f. For the same reason 12: 1–6 is parallel to 2: 19–23, although the names are slightly different through transliteration and metathesis: Bigthan became Gabatha and Teresh became Tharra. The king's name is given by all the English versions of the additions as Artaxerxes, which follows the Greek text, but in the canonical book the name is uniformly given as Ahasuerus, following the Hebrew. The generally accepted opinion is that the king is Xerxes I (485–465) of which name Ahasuerus is one form. The Greek versions almost uniformly throughout the Book and the Additions have Artaxerxes.

In 12: 6 Haman is described as a Bougaean. This word defies explanation beyond the fact that it is also found in the Septuagint of Esther 3: 1, where the Hebrew has Agagite. It is evidently a corruption of some kind within the transmission of the Greek text. The author of the Additions has simply perpetuated a mistake. In 16: 10 Haman is described as a Macedonian, which seems to be due to the Septuagint rendering of 9: 24 where the Hebrew again has Agagite.

In 13: 6 the reference to the slaughter on the fourteenth day is clearly a confusion with the day of the Celebration (Esther 9: 15, 17): the day intended should be the thirteenth (8: 12).

CHAPTER VII

THE BOOK OF WISDOM

THE book falls into three parts:

1. Wisdom in ordinary life and affairs; the obvious advantages of wisdom over against wickedness, chapters 1–6.

2. In praise of divine wisdom, chapters 7–9.

3. The conflict between wisdom and folly as seen in an historical setting, chapters 10–19.

1. Wisdom in ordinary life and affairs

Chapter 1 shows that it is desirable to live a good life dictated by wisdom because God is all-seeing and rewards the righteous with immortality. The author then goes on to refute the position of people such as the Epicureans who say that life is short and sorrowful and that men should make the best of it while they may (2: 1–20). He refutes it by an exposition of the retributive justice of God. It is not an arbitrary retribution, for men receive according to their ways and their thoughts; 'the ungodly will be punished as their reasoning deserves'. The author points out that, though the wicked seem often to prosper and live a long life, they are not necessarily happy, for their end is death and not an easy death at that. For the righteous, on the other hand, there is immortality and the vindication of the judgment day when the unrighteous shall be brought to a realization of their folly and God, like an armed warrior, will fight on behalf of the righteous (2: 21 – 5: 23). Then in chapter 6 there is an appeal to the leaders (who are unspecified but are probably Jewish and ungodly) to pay heed to what the author will go on to say about wisdom for it is wisdom that promotes to a kingdom. Thus by the introduction of wisdom the way is prepared for the central and most important part of the book.

2. *In praise of divine wisdom*

The author assumes the role of king, clearly intended to be Solomon and therefore pseudonymous, and says how he has received the divine gift of wisdom and has been initiated into the secret of things (7: 1–22a). He then describes the wisdom of God as a cosmic and revelatory principle (7: 22b – 8: 1) and goes on to say how he sought to make her his constant companion in life. This he does in terms of courtship and marriage (8: 2–20). The section closes with a prayer to God that he would grant the wisdom that is thus highly to be desired (8: 21 – 9: 18).

3. *The conflict between wisdom and folly, as seen in an historical setting*

These last ten chapters of the book have been described as a 'midrash in glorification of the Jews'[1] and they seek to show that wisdom has constantly been with the chosen and blameless people of Israel and guided them in their history. Four phases of the history are reviewed: the patriarchal age (10: 1–14), in Egypt and during the Exodus (10: 15 – 12: 27; 15: 18 – 17: 21), the age when the craze for idolatry was rife (13: 1 – 15: 17) and finally Israel after the Exodus (18, 19).

[1] Holmes in Charles, *Apocrypha etc.*, Vol. I,

Two ideas are given prominence in these later chapters. The first may be stated by quoting 11:5, 'For through the very things by which their enemies were punished, they themselves received benefit in their need', and the second by 11:16, 'that they might learn that one is punished by the very things by which he sins'. The events of the Exodus and the punishment of the Egyptians are the illustrations given.

THE PLACE OF THE BOOK OF WISDOM IN ISRAEL'S LITERATURE

It is one of the five main works of the Israelite 'wisdom' school, the others being Ecclesiastes, Proverbs, Job and Ecclesiasticus.[1] It is unique among them as being a product of the Alexandrian school. By the first century B.C. the Jewish community in Alexandria was of long and high standing among the dispersed Jews. If tradition is sound the Jews could claim to have been settled in Alexandria by Alexander the Great when he founded the city in 332 B.C. Whether the Jewish community was a royal foundation or not, it was in a favoured and privileged position and had every opportunity to develop a full cultural life of its own. And yet not essentially its own, for its language was Greek and in using that language as the medium of religious thought the members of the community unconsciously, and sometimes perhaps consciously, introduced Greek ideas into their writings. This latter possibility was all the greater in a city like Alexandria where there was a strong academic life in the Greek community and whose philosophical school ranked high among those of the near east. The educated Jew would not only be familiar with the language and literature of Hellenism, he would be in-

[1] There are also a number of 'wisdom' Psalms.

terested also in its ideas, religious, philosophical and ethical. Although couched in different language, the moral ideals of the Greeks were similar to and comparable with those of the Jews. In discussions in the schools and marketplaces the Jews would hear ideas that were already half familiar to them and that would seem to be complementary to those they had learned from their Jewish teachers. They may well have been in danger of finding the less rigid religious principles and practices of the Greeks more attractive than unbending devotion to the precepts of the Mosaic law. The Greeks, for their part, might have shown an interest in a religion which claimed so staunch an adherence to details of everyday observance from its members, but might fail to understand it because its language medium was unknown to them and therefore a serious obstacle in their way.

What would a Jewish writer and teacher wish to do in such a situation? First, for his own people, he would desire to interpret their religious faith in terms of the language they heard and used every day of their lives. Secondly, he would wish to make the Jewish faith more acceptable to Greek scholars and to the intelligentsia generally. It would be natural for him to write in Greek, not only because it was the everyday language of both Greeks and Jews in Alexandria, but also because the Old Testament, or at least most of it, had already been translated into Greek and would be known in that language to practically the whole Jewish community outside Palestine. What he wrote in Greek might make its appeal to both Jew and Greek: to the Jew because it would show that his faith and ideals were neither extraordinary nor barbaric and to the Greek because it would show that the Jews were not lacking in general culture, good sense and sound knowledge.

This is probably why the book of Wisdom came to be written. The author's work is characterized by (i) a knowledge and use of the Old Testament in its Greek form, (ii) a rejection of the outlook of the book of Ecclesiastes in favour of his own point of view, (iii) an unhampered use of Greek idiom and philosophical terms and (iv) the description of the essentially Hebrew idea of wisdom in Greek terms comparable with those which might be used to describe the world pervading spirit.

(i) There are four places where the author so paraphrases or alludes to passages in the Old Testament as to show clear dependence on the Greek translation. 2: 12: 'Let us lie in wait for the righteous man, for he is inconvenient to us' is based on the Greek of Isa. 3: 10; the Hebrew means 'Say of the righteous that it will be well'. 11: 4: 'water was given them out of flinty rock' where the Greek word *akrotomos* properly means 'precipitous' and is dependent upon the Greek of Deut. 8: 15 where the same word translates the Hebrew word for flint. 11: 22: 'Because the whole world before thee is like a speck that tips the scales' is a clear allusion to Isa. 40: 15, 'the nations . . . are accounted as the dust on the scales' where in the LXX the Greek word (*rhopē*) means the turn of the scale. Lastly, 15: 10: 'His heart is ashes' is a reminiscence of LXX of Isa. 44: 20 'know thou that their heart is ashes and they were led astray' where the Hebrew means: 'He feeds on ashes, a deceived heart has turned him aside'.

(ii) In 2: 1–20 the author describes the position of those who say that birth is but a chance, that man will be dispersed at death into thin air and that the only wisdom is to eat, drink and be merry, and to be crowned 'with rosebuds before they wither'. It was in all probability an attack on the Epicureans, but the description of their attitude to

life is couched in terms similar to those found in the book
of Ecclesiastes. This was deliberately done by the author,
who was himself posing as king Solomon in whose name
Ecclesiastes had also been written. He is apparently attempting to bring 'Solomon' up-to-date in the light of a
belief in immortality. The way of life advocated in the
Jewish law gives fullest scope to wisdom and leads to immortal life.

(iii) As far as the limited range of his subject allowed,
coupled with the fact that Greek may have been a second
language for him, the author is unhampered in his use of
Greek, with natural idiom and a wide vocabulary[1] which
included many terms that would be more appropriate in a
philosophical treatise (although we could consider 7: 22 ff.,
where most of them occur, to be a treatise in miniature).
The four cardinal virtues are listed in 8: 7, 'for she teaches
self-control and prudence, justice and courage'. In 6: 17–20
there is a figure of speech known as *sorites* in which the
argument proceeds step by step, repeating the last term
and building it up with a new one. The conclusion is not as
complete as one would expect and it is thought by some
scholars that a member is missing. A logical ending would
run something like 'the beginning of wisdom brings men
nearer to God'.[2] The same figure of speech is to be found
in Romans 5: 3–5 and 8: 30. There is a very free paraphrase
of a passage in Plato[3] in 9: 15:

> For a perishable body weighs down the soul,
> And this earthy tent burdens the thoughtful mind.

---

[1] But there is one error (twice used—4: 12 and 16: 25) in the use of
metalleuō instead of *metallassō*, and one misused word, namely *philo-
psuchos*, used in 11: 26 to mean 'lover of souls'.

[2] A. T. S. Goodrick, *The Book of Wisdom*, 1913, p. 175.

[3] *Phaedo* 81c.

E

When Pseudo-Solomon uses a philosophical phrase in 11 : 17 where he speaks of God creating the world out of 'formless matter' he is using scholastic cliché to build up a more impressive description of God's creative activity but not to suggest that he believes in a dualism of God and matter. The phrase in 17 : 12 that runs : 'For fear is nothing but a surrender of the helps that come from reason' has often been thought to have been in current use in the schools of rhetoric. The conclusion may be drawn that the author was using a language in which he was, for all practical purposes, quite at home and that he was fairly familiar with its philosophical ideas and literature.

(iv) For the first time, so far as we know, in the series of descriptions of divine wisdom (Proverbs, Job, Ecclesiasticus, Wisdom) the language medium is Greek. By a happy chance the word for wisdom in both Hebrew and Greek is feminine; this facilitated the maintenance of the personification, found first in Prov. 8. When the author went on to speak of wisdom in terms of spirit (*pneuma*) he was using a word with a rich connotation and one which already in Greek was used for the all-pervading world spirit. This is probably the nearest pre-Christian approach to the doctrine of the Incarnation, since, as we shall note in the next section, wisdom was thought of as both a cosmic principle and a medium of revelation. It may perhaps be said that the Wisdom conception carries nearly everything that the *logos* doctrine has, except that, being feminine, the idea of Wisdom was necessarily limited and fettered.

DISTINCTIVE IDEAS AND TEACHING OF THE BOOK OF WISDOM

Much of what may be said here is due to the refashioning of Jewish thought in Greek terms. It may be claimed that

the author's chief contribution to Judaism was his attempt
to reconcile Hebrew and Greek thought. Within Judaism
this book is the most notable of such attempts. Within
Christianity St. Paul also attempted to reconcile Hebrew
and Greek thought. It seems extremely probable that Paul
knew the book of Wisdom quite well, or else the community in which he grew up cherished the same fundamental
ideas as that in which the author of Wisdom lived. In two
places Paul has wording that is reminiscent of Wisdom, but
since in each case there is also similarity with passages in
Isaiah it is not possible to say that he was directly dependent on Wisdom. The places in question are: Rom. 9: 19,
20/Wisd. 12: 12/Isa. 29: 16 and Eph. 6: 11–17/Wisd. 5:
18–20/Isa. 59: 17. In the Epistle to the Romans there are
two lines of argument that seem clearly to echo arguments
found in Wisdom. The first, Rom. 1: 18–32, speaks of the
deliberate rejection of natural religion and knowledge of
God and the consequent resort to idols with its train of
moral degradation. This is very much in line with the
argument in Wisd. 12–14 which also includes a catalogue
of moral evils (14: 25 ff.). The second, 9: 19–23, incorporates three of the main arguments of the last part of Wisdom, chapters 10–19, namely (1) the impossibility of resisting the divine power, (2) the forbearance of God and (3) the
analogy of the potter. But the difference between the two
writers is as fundamental as the similarity. The author of
Wisdom remained an ardent nationalist; God's forbearance towards the Gentiles was temporary only and its
primary value was as instruction and example for the
Jewish people. St. Paul's Christian sympathy embraced the
whole world: between the two writers lay the Incarnation.

The main modifications which the author's Greek interests caused him to introduce into Jewish doctrine may

be seen in the idea of man, the hope of immortality and the conception of divine wisdom.

(a) *The idea of man*. It is well known that the Old Testament idea of man was, broadly speaking, that of an animated body: the flesh was formed and into it was breathed the life-giving breath or spirit; thus man became a living person. In Hebrew literature there are four terms—flesh, spirit, heart and soul—that are commonly used in speaking of man's being. Often they are spoken of as if they had a semi-independent nature of their own but they remain part and parcel of the unity that is man and at death 'the dust returns to the earth as it was, and the spirit returns to God who gave it' (Eccles. 12: 7). At times the author of Wisdom lives in the same world, for instance he thus speaks of death: 'this man who was made of earth a short time before and after a little while goes to the earth from which he was taken, when he is required to return the soul that was lent him' (15: 8). But whatever may be said about the basic unity of man, the terms themselves are distinct, and constant use of them as if they spoke of separate parts of man, coupled with the fact that Greek thought used much the same terms but distinguished between the body which was of the earth and the soul or spirit which was pre-existent and immortal, meant that men came to regard the different parts of man as distinct and separable. It was easy therefore for the author to write:

For a perishable body weighs down the soul,
And this earthy tent burdens the thoughtful mind (9: 15).

In the previous chapter there is a sentence (8: 19 f.) in which the author seems to begin with a Jewish sentiment, 'As a child I was by nature well endowed, and a good soul fell to my lot' where the emphasis lies on the body as the seat of self-hood, but he immediately seems to correct this to be in line with current Greek thought: 'Or rather, being good, I entered an undefiled body', in which phrase the fundamental element of self-hood is the soul which entered an earthly body. Such passages ought not to be pressed too far, but it does look as though the author is definitely departing from the Hebrew emphasis on the body animated by God and leaning towards an idea of the separate entity of the soul imprisoned for a time in a body which was not always as good as it might be. If this was so, it need not surprise us that he holds a doctrine of immortality more firmly than any previous Jewish writer.

(b) *The hope of immortality.* The author of Wisdom stands well inside that section of Jewish belief which saw a solution of the problem of retribution and of innocent suffering in the belief in a life after death. The belief had been formulated only twice in canonical literature, Isa. 26: 19, and Dn. 12: 2, although there had been a yearning for it expressed by Job and a glimpse of its nature and possibility in Psalm 73.

To the impious he ascribes the belief that death ends everything: 'When it is extinguished, the body will turn to ashes, and the spirit will dissolve into empty air' (2: 3). Since this is what they believe, and they have also made a covenant with death (1: 16 cf. Isa. 28: 15, 18), they will certainly die. They will not, however, thereby escape the punishment they deserve. It will begin to be worked out in their lifetime: 'one is punished by the very things by which he sins' (11: 16). They will see the vindication of the righteous, with God fighting on their behalf, and at the judgment day they will be convicted of their sins (4: 20). The righteous, on the other hand, will enjoy everlasting life, 'for God created man for incorruption, and made him in the image of his own eternity' (2: 23). This is a commentary on Gen. 1: 26, based on Greek thought, which holds that immortality is one of the essential attributes of deity. 'God did not make death, and he does not delight in the death of the living' (1: 13); with this as a fundamental element in his creed he can go on to say (in 3: 1): 'But the souls of the righteous are in the hand of God, and no torment will ever touch them'. It does not matter whether we regard this as springing from the author's Hebrew background and interpret 'soul' in the sense of 'person', or as springing from his Greek environment and take 'soul' to mean the spiritual and immortal element in a man: in either case the meaning in the context is clear; the righteous will be cared for by God and will receive a blessed immortality as the reward of their goodness.

(c) *The conception of divine wisdom.* We have already mentioned that the very fact of its expression in Greek terms was likely to modify the conception. To understand the position of the book of Wisdom in the development of the conception we must first review its earlier forms. It emerged suddenly and unheralded in the book of Proverbs 8, where the wisdom of God is personified as a woman who was at God's side at creation, who is the source of all sound wisdom in men and who can be wooed and won by them. Within the limits of the Old Testament canon it occurs again, not so clearly personified, in Job 28. It is essentially God's prerogative; men must observe religious life and practice so that wisdom may be granted to them. Before we turn to look briefly at the development in the Apocrypha it may be well to ask where the idea originated. Proverbs and Job are both too early to suppose that it came into Hebrew thought through Greek influence, although once the idea was firmly rooted its further develop-

ment was undoubtedly due to Hebrew familiarity with
Greek thought. Its sudden emergence has been thought to
imply that it came into Judaism from outside and in that
case the nearest counterpart would be Asha, one of the six
heavenly intermediaries of Ahura Mazda in Iranian religion.[1] Asha, called 'truth' by Plutarch, represented
purity and all the religious and moral duties of man. This
is an attractive theory, but if, as we shall see, there is reason for thinking that the idea may have been a native
growth, it may be that the Persian system only influenced
the idea in its later development along the lines of hypostasis.[2] On the other hand a strong case could be made for
assuming it to have been an independent growth within
Judaism. There was a persistent Semitic tradition of belief
in consort goddesses. One of the sins to which the Israelites
were prone in the time of Jeremiah and Ezekiel, and indeed
at other times, was that of worshipping the Queen of
Heaven. The wisdom figure may be a deliberate adaptation
of this in order to counteract its danger. Wisdom is feminine and invites men to her house to get wisdom and understanding, as the goddess might do. She is the darling of
Yahweh (Prov. 8: 30). The ideas of the Word of God and
the Spirit of God, though somewhat different in function,
may have helped to shape the conception of wisdom. The
word for wisdom in both Hebrew and Greek is feminine
and therefore makes female personification all the easier.
It came into use at a time when there was a growing appreciation of God's transcendence and we may suppose that
the desire for a mediatory principle between the world and
God was a subsidiary factor in its development. Whatever
its origin, it came to stay for at least three centuries and

[1] O. S. Rankin, *Israel's Wisdom Literature*, 1936.
[2] W. Eichrodt, *Theologie des Alten Testaments*, vol. 2, 1935, p. 41 n.

left its mark on the shaping of both Jewish and Christian theology.

After Proverbs and Job we next meet with an exposition of it in Ecclesiasticus 24 written at about 180 B.C. Whereas in Proverbs the figure is probably nothing more than personification of wisdom, it is almost certain that ben Sira wrote of it in terms amounting nearly, if not quite, to hypostasis. She (wisdom) was created from the beginning and was to be eternal: she came forth from the mouth of the Most High and covered the earth as a mist, that is, as did the spirit at creation. She sought a dwelling on earth and ultimately took root in the Lord's own inheritance, Israel. At the end of the description ben Sira goes on to say: 'All this is the book of the covenant of the Most High God, the law which Moses commanded us'. Not only does this identification with the law indicate the supreme place held by the law in the esteem of the Jews but it suggests that ben Sira regarded wisdom as a principle of revelation as well as a principle of creation. Moreover, the law, though of divine origin, had been sent to Israel through Moses and was Israel's treasured possession, that is to say, nothing could rob it of its self-existence in the eyes of its adherents. It may be claimed that in thus identifying wisdom with the law ben Sira was treating wisdom as a hypostasis originating in and from God but becoming distinct from him and in a manner independent of him. When the author of Wisdom takes up the conception, probably a hundred years later, wisdom remains a principle both of revelation and of creation, but the hypostasization is carried through more completely. She was present when God was making the world, and pervades and penetrates all things by reason of her pureness, being a breath of the power of God and a pure emanation of the glory of the Almighty. She can do all things, and while remaining in herself, she renews all things; in every generation she passes into holy souls and makes them friends of God and prophets. 'Solomon' prays God to 'send her forth from the holy heavens . . . that she may be with me'. Later in the same prayer (9: 17) there is an implicit identification of wisdom and spirit: 'Who has learned thy counsel, unless thou hast given wisdom and sent thy holy Spirit from on high?'

When the author thus associates wisdom with spirit and in other places 'describes this world-pervading wisdom as a *pneuma*, it is quite impossible that he was not consciously reproducing current Stoic language about the *pneuma* which was also a peculiarly pure and subtle fire, identical with God, which penetrated all the kosmos and ordered everything with perfect wisdom, which, lastly, constituted the reason in man and made those obedient to it sages and friends of God'.[1]

AUTHORSHIP, PURPOSE, DATE AND PLACE OF ORIGIN

Three chapters of the book make a clear claim to have been written by Solomon (chh. 7–9). The opening words of chapter 7 are cast as the words of a king while 9: 8 makes the intention clear: 'Thou hast given command to build a temple on thy holy mountain . . .'. Mention has already been made of the use of pseudonyms in apocalyptic writing,[2] but the practice was not limited to such writers. It had become traditional to trace all laws back to Moses and therefore to ascribe them to him, and psalms were readily ascribed to David. Solomon was the figure-head of wisdom literature and all inspiration of wisdom might be thought of as being in direct line of succession to him. The author

---

[1] Edwyn Bevan, *Symbolism and Belief*, 1938, pp. 185f.
[2] See on II Esdras.

may have been the more ready to use the pseudonym because he seems to have wished to correct the representation of Solomon that is found in Ecclesiastes. The English
title to the book follows the Vulgate, but the Greek has
'The Wisdom of Solomon'. In the Syriac version there is a
longer title: 'The book of the great wisdom of Solomon,
son of David; of which there is a doubt, whether another
wise man of the Hebrews wrote it in a prophetic spirit,
putting it in the name of Solomon, and it was received'.
The actual authorship is, unfortunately, completely concealed in the pseudonym. Anything else that may be said
about authorship is by way of deduction. Some early
Christian writers, for instance, Jerome, and possibly the
Greek archetype of the Muratorian fragment, attributed
the book to Philo (*c.* 30 B.C.–A.D. 45) but whatever similarities the book might show to the writings of Philo they
are far outweighed by the fact that there is no trace of the
allegorical interpretation of scripture that was so typical of
Philo and there is nothing at all about the *logos* conception.

Whoever the author was, his book is a Jewish apologetic
addressed to men whose habit of life and thought was
Greek. Whether they were Greeks by race or whether they
were Greek-speaking Jews is not so easy to determine. In
view of the strongly nationalistic note in the third part of
the book it is usually thought that the people to whom it
was addressed were Jews. What is said of the Egyptians
and Canaanites in the last chapters of the book, of their
sins and consequent punishment, of the innate evil of the
Canaanites and their refusal of the mercy of God offered to
them, when compared with what is said about the blame-
lessness and loyalty of the Jews, does not commend itself
as the natural way to present Jewish apologetic to non-
Jews, even though they be neither Egyptian nor Canaanite.

The rulers who are addressed in 1: 1, 6: 1–3, 9 might be thought to be highly placed Jewish apostates who owed their position perhaps to their acceptance of Greek manners and customs. There were such men; we know of Tiberius Alexander, a nephew of Philo, who was Governor of Alexandria at the time of Nero. If this is so the unlawful unions referred to in 3: 16 and 4: 6 may be mixed marriages which were strongly condemned by pious Jews and whose offspring were known as *mamzerim* (bastards). If the author had these men chiefly in mind we cannot rule out the possibility that he hoped his book would reach a wider circle. It may well be that he wrote 12: 19 urging that the righteous were to be *philanthropos*, 'kind, humane', to combat the reproach that the Jews were *hostes humani generis*.

The language and ideas of the book point to a strong Jewish centre in a Hellenistic city as its place of origin. Alexandria is the natural city to think of; it was a centre of Greek culture with its schools of philosophy, and it had the largest body of Jewish residents outside Palestine. The choice of the Exodus period by way of illustration in the last chapters of the book, with its inevitable references to Egypt and the Egyptians, could be regarded as some support for an Egyptian place of origin.

There is no clear indication of date in the book, but there are several approaches towards an approximate date. First, its relation to the Old Testament and other Jewish literature shows it to be not earlier than the middle of the second century B.C. It shows knowledge of one of the latest of Old Testament books, Daniel (3: 8), and, as we have seen, used the Greek version of some of the other books. In its discussion of Wisdom it is the natural successor to Ecclesiasticus, which is usually dated *c*. 180 B.C. The idea of immortality is certainly no earlier than that of Daniel and maybe

somewhat later in development. Second, if Paul's dependence on it, or at least knowledge of it, in Romans be accepted (and it can hardly come after Paul, since it is less
mature) the book must have been written earlier than
Romans, that is, earlier than A.D. 58. But its relation to
Philo brings it earlier still. There is nothing in Wisdom of
the characteristic ideas, thoughts and methods of Philo,
nothing at all about the *logos* conception and only the
barest hint (10: 17), if that, of an allegorical interpretation
of the Old Testament. These arguments bring us to some-
where within a period of 150 years, i.e. from 150 B.C. to the
turn of the era. It has been described as 'the solitary survival from the wreck of the earlier works of the philosophical school of Alexandria which culminated in Philo the
contemporary of our Lord'.[1]

It is thus the latest product of the canonical and apocryphal wisdom literature and is probably the only representative of that literature to have been written entirely
outside Palestine in the Dispersion. It is transitional:
Greek has entirely taken the place of Hebrew as the language of scholarship, but Jewish particularism is still holding its head high and will not give place to the universalism
that is instinct in the Wisdom conception and which finally
came into its own in the New Testament.

[1] H. B. Swete, *Introduction to the Old Testament in Greek*, 2nd ed. 1914,
p. 269. Attempts have been made to define the date more closely.
H. St. J. Thackeray, *Grammar of the Old Testament in Greek*, 1909, p. 62
arguing from linguistic uses places it in the same period as the translation of Ecclesiasticus, *c.* 132 B.C. A. T. S. Goodrick, *The Book of Wisdom*,
1913, thinks that the passage about image worship in 14: 16, 17 may
refer to the attempt of Caligula to have his image erected in Jerusalem
for Jews to worship in 41 A.D. The reference however is couched in quite
general terms and could have Greek emperor worship as its background
quite as naturally as the Roman emperor worship.

CHAPTER VIII

ECCLESIASTICUS

OR

THE WISDOM OF JESUS BEN SIRA[1]

THE title ECCLESIASTICUS which is customary in our English versions comes from the Vulgate and has been in use at least since the time of Cyprian (d. A.D. 258). The title was either modelled on Ecclesiastes or was given to it because it had become a well-loved book in the church and came to be called the church-book. The Vatican MS of the Greek gives the title simply as *Sophia Seirach*, which is where the alternative form, Sirach, of the proper name comes from. The *ch* makes the Hebrew guttural firmer than it need be, and present-day usage in giving the name of the author is to follow the Hebrew more closely with the form ben Sira. The form Sirach is sometimes used in giving the title of the book.

CONTENTS

It is practically impossible to give an adequate summary of the contents, because there is no sustained sequence of narrative or argument. For the most part it consists of moral and religious proverbs and maxims with an occasional expansion of theme into short essays. No clear sys-

---

[1] In A.V. and R.V. the title runs: The Wisdom of Jesus the son of Sirach, or Ecclesiasticus; in R.S.V. Ecclesiasticus, or the Wisdom of Jesus the Son of Sirach.

tem of selection or of arrangement is discernible. Conformity of subject matter probably had a lot to do with the order. This is clearly so in the case of 36: 1–17, which is a prayer for mercy and is placed where it is because chapter 35 ends:

> And the Lord will not delay . . .
> Till he judges the case of his people
> And makes them rejoice in his mercy.
> Mercy is as welcome when he afflicts them
> As clouds of rain in the time of drought.

Mercy is the common connecting link.

There are, however, a number of places throughout the book where a fresh start to a theme is made, and the book may be divided into sections according to these new beginnings. It is not improbable that they reflect the author's teaching method and that each section represents one section either of oral teaching or of writing. An example of such a fresh start may be seen at 16: 24 f.:

> Listen to me, my son, and acquire knowledge,
> And pay close attention to my words.
> I will impart instruction by weight,
> And declare knowledge accurately.

He then goes on to describe the wisdom of God in creation. On this basis the following sections may be distinguished in the book:

Prologue (which falls outside the verse numbering) by the author's grandson saying that he thought his grandfather's book was worth translating but that he craved the reader's indulgence because he knew that translations did not always convey the sense of the original.

Section 1: 1: 1 – 16: 23. Wisdom is the Lord's but men

may begin to possess her if they will have true religion and fear of the Lord. Then there follows a number of maxims setting out the kind of behaviour most consonant with the pursuit of wisdom. Two further paragraphs in praise of wisdom occur within the section, namely, 4: 11–19 and 14: 20 – 15: 8.

Section 2: 16: 24 – 23: 27. The divine wisdom in creation sets the pattern for human wisdom. Various moral precepts are added.

Section 3: 24: 1 – 33: 18.[1] This section begins with a hymn in praise of wisdom (24: 1–29) and then goes on to give many wise sayings about men's behaviour as dictated by wisdom.

Section 4: 33: 19 – 36: 17. Sundry precepts about wisdom in religious and in secular affairs.

Section 5: 36: 18 – 39: 11. Rules about social life, health and sickness. The section closes with an essay on the privileges of a scribe's (statesman's) vocation as compared with certain craftsmen, farmer, engraver of gems, smith, potter.

Section 6: 39: 12 – 42: 14. A hymn of praise to God, followed by precepts and comments of various kinds.

Section 7: 42: 15 – 43: 33. An essay in praise of the wonders of creation.

Section 8: 44: 1 – 50: 29. An essay in praise of the famous men in Israel's history.

Epilogue: 51: 1–30, in which the author begins by praising God for his help, then goes on to say how he sought for wisdom till he found her and finally summons others to hear him and learn from him in his school.

[1] Pfeiffer, *op. cit.*, p. 353, suggests that the book was published in two parts: 1–23 and 24–end, each part beginning with praise of Wisdom.

LANGUAGE

The author's grandson tells us that he translated his grandfather's book (from Hebrew) into Greek. For centuries there was no trace of the Hebrew original, but in 1896 a sheet of parchment containing 39: 15 – 40: 7 was discovered. Thereafter further parts of the same MS and parts of four other MSS of the book were discovered and found to have come from the same ultimate source, the Genizah of the Ezra Synagogue in Cairo. Altogether some two-thirds of the Hebrew text is now known to be extant.[1] To these parts from the Cairo Genizah we may now add fragments from Qumrân, Cave II, representing Ecclus. 6: 20–31.[2] Differences between the Hebrew fragments themselves, and between them and the Greek and Syriac, as well as differences between the Greek MSS, offer useful material for text criticism and show how slight changes might creep into texts during the processes of copying and transmission. Not only so, but there are some longer additions, both in one form of the Greek and in some of the Hebrew fragments, which suggest that scribes were not averse to making 'improvements' in the text if they thought them desirable. The nature of such additions can be seen by reading them as printed in the footnotes of the Revised Standard Version. The Authorized Version is based on the longer form of the Greek text and has these additions within its text; the Revised Version omits them and draws attention to their omission in the margin.[3]

[1] A useful edition of the Hebrew text is that by Lévi in Semitic Study Series, No. III. *The Hebrew Text of the Book of Ecclesiasticus*, 1904.

[2] J. T. Milik, *Ten Years of Discovery in the Wilderness of Judaea*, 1959, p. 32.

[3] The translation given in Charles' *Apocrypha etc.* is based on the Hebrew wherever that is extant.

DATE

The book is usually thought to have been written in about 180 B.C. This is largely based on the fact that the grandson in his prologue says that he went to Egypt in the thirty-eighth year of Euergetes and that he set to work translating the book some time afterwards. This must refer to Euergetes II, 170–116 B.C. (Euergetes I did not rule long enough to reach the thirty-eighth year). If the grandson went to Egypt in 132 it might be reasonable to think of the grandfather as being active about fifty years earlier. The eulogy on Simon son of Onias in chapter 50 gives some confirmation of the date, although it must be admitted that information about Simon is scanty. He is mentioned, in passing, in Josephus (Antiquities, XII. iv. 10) and in later tradition (Mishnah and Talmud) his high-priesthood ranked as one of the more glorious periods of Israel's history. The repairs and fortifications to which ben Sira alludes (50: 1–4) were probably necessary after Antiochus the Great began his invasion of Palestine (201 B.C.). There is no certain evidence that Antiochus actually attacked Jerusalem.

THE AUTHOR

His name is given in 50: 27 as Jesus son of Sira son of Eleazar, and the prologue has 'my grandfather Jesus'. All else that we can learn of him has to be gleaned from the few personal references that he himself makes in his book and from his subject matter and manner of treatment. He belonged to that class in Israel whom Jeremiah called 'the wise' (Jer. 18: 18), but he was also a scribe and was in his element in holding up the scribe's vocation as the noblest of all (chh. 38, 39). Although the use of the term is an

F

anachronism, ben Sira has been described as Sadducaean in outlook. This is because, like the Sadducees, he placed an emphasis on the scriptures and was interested in the Temple and its services, and at the same time he shows no trace of those beliefs which characterized the Pharisees— angels and demons, survival after death. It has become traditional to associate scribes with Pharisees, but that is by no means inevitable; the priestly aristocracy studied the scriptures as zealously as any Pharisee might, and this study would be fostered by like-minded scribes. If this is the tradition in which ben Sira stood there is one curious fact about his essay on Israel's famous men; it has no mention whatever of Ezra. It may be that ben Sira felt that Ezra's work was eclipsed in that generation by Nehemiah's work.[1] We may assume that he had travelled widely, encountering dangers on his journeys (34: 11, 12) and moved freely in the higher strata of society (39: 4). He was zealous for the Temple and its services and only those kings who had some association with the worship of the Temple are singled out by name for special mention. David for establishing the temple music, and Hezekiah and Josiah for their zeal in the reformation of the worship and cultus (49: 4). He shows special interest in Aaron as the first of the priests and in Simon as the last up to the time of writing: Phinehas also is praised because of his zeal in the fear of the Lord (45: 23). His search for wisdom was probably purely 'academic' to begin with, but the more he studied the more he was constrained to teach.

I went forth like a canal from a river
And like a water channel into a garden.

---

[1] Cf. the apparent neglect of Nehemiah, to the greater fame of Ezra in I Esdras.

I said: 'I will water my orchard and drench my garden
  plot';
And lo, my canal became a river, and my river became a
  sea.
I will again make instruction shine forth like the dawn,
  and I will make it shine afar. (24: 30–32)

Eventually he had a school of instruction in his own house
and invited all to it without charge:

> Draw near to me, you who are untaught,
>   And lodge in my school. . . .
> I opened my mouth and said,
>   Get these things for yourselves without money.
>   (51: 23, 25)

He lived at a time when more and more Jews were becoming interested in the culture of the Greeks under whose
rule they were living, but he shows not the slightest trace
of Greek thought, reflecting mainly traditional Judaism to
which many still clung and from which there sprang the
forces that regained religious freedom in 165 B.C.

Ben Sira undoubtedly rendered his own generation a
great service in giving expression to the beliefs and practices of the sincere and devout Jews who were the very
core of their nation. It may well be that his book helped to
strengthen the faith and courage of those who were called
upon to resist oppression and persecution under Antiochus
Epiphanes and to fight for their religious freedom. Certainly when the Maccabean wars were at an end his grandson thought the book was still relevant and translated it
into Greek for the sake of the many Jews who were dispersed from their national home. To the historian it is
useful in that it presents a sober picture of a cross section
of Jerusalem's population written by one who, so far as we

can tell, had no axe to grind, but had only a genuine urge to teach true doctrine.

In two respects the picture goes further than that of a representative cross section of Jerusalem society. It has something more to say on the conception of the wisdom of God than Proverbs 8 had, and in the essay on Israel's famous men it has a fresh approach to the Biblical story. Ben Sira's contribution to the development of the conception of divine wisdom is found in chapter 24. In previous chapters he had written the usual things about the fear of the Lord being the beginning of wisdom (1: 14) and of how God would give her to those who kept the commandments (1: 26), although when a man had obtained wisdom from God it was not so much to give him a marked skill in craftsmanship, as to give him greater capacity to observe the law. Then in chapter 24 he describes divine wisdom as if she herself were speaking. To begin with the picture is very much the same as that of Proverbs 8. Wisdom was the first of created things, was with God from the beginning, aided him in creation and then took up a dwelling with Israel after seeking elsewhere in vain. This description virtually absorbs two familiar Old Testament conceptions. 24: 3 reads:

> I came forth from the mouth of the Most High,
> And covered the earth like a mist

which is reminiscent of the spirit of God brooding over the face of the waters at creation. Secondly it takes up the idea of the creative word, for wisdom does here everything that God's spoken word was thought to do. Although wisdom's creative work was first in time, her work in revelation was first in importance and when she had scoured the world for a resting-place she was commanded to pitch her tent in

Israel. Here ben Sira brings his peculiar contribution to
the conception of wisdom, for it is in Jerusalem and in the
Temple that wisdom has her home and, in fact, she is to be
identified with the 'book of the covenant of the Most High
God, the law which Moses commanded' (24: 23). This was
natural and well-nigh inevitable.[1] By ben Sira's time the
Law had assumed highest authority as the word of God to
his people. It was the supreme revelation, and if wisdom
was thought to be the medium of revelation then the two
must somehow be in organic relationship. Moreover, the
only way to wisdom for man lay in observing the Law:

> Reflect on the statutes of the Lord,
> And meditate at all times on his commandments.
> It is he who will give insight to your mind,
> And your desire for wisdom will be granted. (6: 37)

In thus identifying wisdom with the Law it may well be
thought that ben Sira has advanced beyond mere personification in his conception of divine wisdom. Wisdom
is, as it were, released by God to take her place, as the Law
had done, in the world of men. This comes very close to
the hypostasizing of wisdom by the author of *Wisdom*
some hundred years later.

It was no new thing to rehearse the past history of
Israel, which is what ben Sira did, among other things, in
his essay on famous men. We find such rehearsals in
Psalms 78, 105 and 106, and later than ben Sira in Wisd.
10, 11; 1 Macc. 2: 51–68; Heb. 11. It was a new thing to
attempt, as he seems to have done, to cover the whole
history and he is more concerned with the men who played
their part in it than in the history itself. This is because he
is continuing his hymn of praise to God, and having sung

[1] They are also identified in Baruch 4: 1.

his praise for the power manifested in the natural world he
turns to the world of men and shows how they praise God
by their obedience. With one possible exception[1] he followed the order of the Hebrew Bible in so far as it existed
in his day. Daniel, of course, had yet to be written, and the
third part of the Canon, the Writings, were still in process
of collection. A careful reading of these chapters, 44–49,
reveals a great deal about the Canon of the Old Testament
as ben Sira understood it. He implies that already there
was a three-fold division, both in an earlier passage, 39: 1
where wisdom, law and prophecies are mentioned together,
and in 44: 3–5 where prophecies and instructions of wise
men are distinguished. Half a century or so later his grandson wrote of the 'law and the prophets and the other books
of our fathers'. As we know from the existence of the
Samaritan Pentateuch, the Law was fixed in its present
form well before ben Sira wrote. The prophets, which in
the Hebrew canon means the historical books as well
(Joshua—2 Kings, the 'former prophets'), were also very
much as we have them. It is clear that when he says that
Isaiah 'comforted those who mourned in Zion' (48: 24) the
book called Isaiah already had chapters 40 ff. joined to it.
The twelve minor prophets were apparently a recognized
group, as they are today, and of them he wrote:

> May the bones of the twelve prophets
> Revive from where they lie,
> For they comforted the people of Jacob
> And delivered them with confident hope. (49: 10)

Ben Sira's interest lay primarily in the Temple and its
services. Aaron received a longer description than Moses

---

[1] The exception is Job, who is mentioned, in the Hebrew text, immediately after Ezekiel (49: 8, 9).

and it is rounded off by reference to the covenant of peace with Aaron and his descendents comparable with that which was established with David (45: 24, 25). David's importance lay as much in the tradition that he established the services and music of the sanctuary as in his prowess as warrior and king. Apart from David and Solomon only two kings are mentioned, Hezekiah and Josiah, both of whom reformed the Temple and its worship. If the omission of the other kings implies condemnation of their religious and moral behaviour then ben Sira was only doing to a greater degree what the Chronicler had done before him. The book of Kings had recorded that six of the kings not named in Ecclesiasticus had done what was right in God's eyes, but the Chronicler had reduced that number to two only, Asa and Jehoshaphat. Ben Sira ignored these also. What is more interesting, however, is that for him the course of history was more dependent on a succession of prophets than of kings. Samuel receives full notice, but Saul is completely passed over. The account of David is prefaced by the words 'And after him [i.e. Samuel] Nathan rose up to prophesy in the days of David' (47: 1). Hezekiah is subordinated to Isaiah (48: 22).

There are some striking omissions in the list. Joseph receives only a passing reference in 49: 15, simply drawing attention to the fact that no man like Joseph had been born. This makes the omission of Daniel all the more noteworthy, for if ben Sira had known the book of Daniel he would have regarded Daniel as being very much like Joseph.[1] The first king, Saul, is not mentioned: the reason for this is not very far to seek; Samuel eclipsed him in ben

[1] This may be thought to confirm the accepted date of Daniel, i.e. as a product of the Maccabean Age, or alternately, if the date of Daniel be now regarded as axiomatic it confirms a date for ben Sira before 165 B.C.

Sira's eyes even to the extent of defeating the enemies, by prayer and sacrifice, that history assigns to Saul. It remains a mystery why ben Sira did not include Ezra in his list. One would have thought that the figure of Ezra the priest-scribe would appeal to a scribe who also had a keen interest in the worship of the Temple. It is possible that in certain circles, such as that to which ben Sira belonged, the work of Nehemiah was regarded as far more important and significant than that of Ezra; their work may even have been merged into the achievement of a single man, in this case Nehemiah. We have seen that the opposite seems to have happened in I Esdras where Ezra's work is all important and Nehemiah is not mentioned, except, perhaps, under a pseudonym or an official title (see on p. 15).

In view of the fact that the third section of the Canon, the Writings, was still unformed as a collection of sacred writings, and at least one book, Daniel, had not as yet been written, it is not surprising to find no allusion to Ruth, Lamentations, Esther, Canticles and Ecclesiastes. In his absorbing interest in the Temple and its services ben Sira is in full sympathy with the Chronicler with whose work he was probably familiar, since in the details of Hezekiah's fortification he follows the account in Chronicles as well as that in Kings.

We may close this account of Ecclesiasticus by setting out in broad outline the ideas and beliefs which ben Sira shared with his contemporaries and which may be considered to be representative of the orthodox Judaism of the first half of the second century B.C. God is personal; not only is he creator, but also a merciful father (23: 1, 18: 13, 14) who pours out his wisdom upon those who love him (1: 10). Those who love him are the Israelites whose God he is and to whom he gave a full revelation through his

wisdom and his law (24: 8, 23). In this conception of the
mediatory nature of wisdom and law ben Sira is reflecting
the growing sense in Israel of the transcendence of God.
This sense of God's aloofness is more marked in post-
Biblical and apocryphal works than it is within the Old
Testament itself. God created the world, but wisdom was
his instrument; God chose Israel to be his own people, but
it was wisdom whom he sent to 'dwell' among them. Men
are urged to stand in awe of God and not to seek to understand things that are far beyond their reach or understanding (3: 17–24).

Even so, God is ready to help those who fear him (2: 1–
6), is merciful to forgive sins and to save in time of affliction (2: 7–11), but men must not presume on his mercy and
forgiveness 'for both mercy and wrath are with him, and
his anger rests on sinners' (5: 6). A man who is a 'father' to
orphans and a 'husband' to their mother, will be like a son
to God (4: 1–10). This stands nearer to New Testament
teaching than does the national 'sonship' of Hosea 11: 1.
One might think that such an attitude would have lifted
ben Sira above the level of nationalism and led him to think
in terms of universalism as did some of the prophets before
him. That was evidently far more than the ordinary Jew
could reach. Israel was God's elect people and it was to
save them that God sent deliverers, as ben Sira says of
Joshua,

> He became, in accordance with his name,
> A great saviour of God's elect. (46: 1)

A further limitation in the thought of the book is that it is
intended for men, women being of no account. Although
the Old Testament story includes women like Deborah,
Jael, Rahab and Esther, to mention only four, ben Sira's

essay on famous men makes no mention of any woman.
One of the sections of the book could almost be headed
'Woman as a source of trouble' (42: 9–14). In 25: 24 he
wrote:

> From a woman sin had its beginning,
> And because of her we all die.

This reflects both his attitude towards woman and towards the fate of man. Death comes to all and is inevitable:

> O death, how bitter is the reminder of you
> To one who lives at peace among his possessions. . . .
> O death, how welcome is your sentence
> To one who is in need and is failing in strength. . . .
>
> (41: 1, 2)

There is no life after death and all that a man can live and
work for is that he shall live on in his good name and in his
children:

> There are some of them who have left a name,
> So that men declare their praise. . . .
> Their posterity will continue for ever,
> And their glory will not be blotted out. (44: 8, 13)

His attitude to death simply reflects that of the Old Testament in general:

Do not fear the sentence of death;
Remember your former days and the end of life;
This is the decree from the Lord for all flesh,
And how can you reject the good pleasure of the Most
    High?
Whether life is for ten or a hundred or a thousand years,
There is no inquiry about it in Hades. (41: 3, 4)

CHAPTER IX

BARUCH

THE book begins with a seemingly explicit date, 'in the fifth year, on the seventh day of the month, at the time when the Chaldeans took Jerusalem and burned it with fire'. At this time Baruch wrote a book which he read before Jeconiah and the other exiles (1: 1–4). Then he collected money and sent the money and the book, with a covering note, to Jehoiakim the high-priest in Jerusalem (1: 5–7). Baruch also took the Temple vessels to return them to Jerusalem (1: 8, 9; this is parenthetical and does not connect with what precedes it or with what follows it). The letter begins with a note that the money is to buy material for sacrifices so that they may sacrifice and pray both for Nebuchadnezzar and his son Belshazzar and for the Exiles who live under them so that God's anger may be turned away. They are then to read the book and make confession (1: 10–14). The confession is that it is through their own sins and disobedience that the calamities have come upon them (1: 15 – 2: 10). At this point there is an abrupt change and what follows is a confession by the exiles of their sin and of their failure to accept the advice of Jeremiah and serve the king of Babylon (2: 11 – 3: 8).

There follows a poem in praise of wisdom. She is God's prerogative and no man, whether prince, warrior, merchant or raconteur, has found her. God alone knows her and has given her to Israel, in fact, she is the whole law of

God (3: 9 – 4: 4). In the next section Jerusalem laments over the present calamity and mourns the loss of her sons (4: 5–16); she is powerless to help them but trusts that the everlasting God will do so (4: 17–29). Then Jerusalem herself is comforted and is promised the return of her children (4: 30 – 5: 9).

Short as it is, the book of Baruch is not a unity. There are at least three distinct parts:[1]

1. A prose section, 1: 1 – 3: 8, which contains the introduction to the book and the confessions of sin by both the Jews in Palestine and the Exiles in Babylon. There is a good deal of dependence on Jeremiah in this section and in one place, 2: 8–19, the phrasing closely follows that of the prayer in Daniel 9: 4–19.

2. A poem in praise of wisdom 3: 9 – 4: 4 which, though short, shows affinities with each of the previous discussions of wisdom, Job 28, Prov. 8, Wisd. 7, 8, Ecclus. 24.

3. A section in verse containing lament over and comfort for Jerusalem; it is very strongly reminiscent in its language of Deutero-Isaiah and in one passage, 5: 5–9 [4: 36 – 5: 9], is dependent on Psalms of Solomon 11: 2–7.

These three sections are probably to be regarded as originally quite independent of each other and collected by an editor. This may account for the difficulties raised by the introduction in 1: 1–9, which may have grown as the book was compiled. There are two main difficulties in it; first, that its sequence is broken by verses 8 and 9, and second, that one cannot say for certain which parts of what follows belong to the letter and which to the book which the letter was said to accompany. The letter cer-

[1] Some scholars divide it into four (1: 1–3 + 3: 9–4: 4; 1: 4–14; 1: 15 – 3: 8; 4: 5 – 5: 9) see Pfeiffer, *op. cit.*, p. 413.

tainly contained 1:10–14. As Baruch now stands the 'book' was probably intended to refer to the rest of it, i.e. 1:15– 5:9; but it is strangely disjointed for a book such as that mentioned in 1:1, 3, 14. There are three other possibilities as to the contents of the book: (i) the confessions contained in 1:15 – 3:18; (ii) the wisdom poem, 3:9 – 4:4; and (iii) the final section of lament and comfort, 4:5 – 5:9. Of these the first is the most probable, although the sudden change from those in Judaea to those still in Babylon is unexpected. On the other hand, the letter itself may have contained 1:10 – 3:8, in which case the wisdom poem would almost certainly be the book referred to.

A further mark of cleavage between the component documents of Baruch may be seen if we compare 1:11, where the people are instructed to pray for Nebuchadnezzar and Belshazzar, with 4:31–34, where utter destruction is promised for those who afflicted Israel and for the city to which they were led captive (cf. also 4:25).

DATE

The book is dated in the fifth year (1:2) at the time when Jerusalem was captured and burnt. If that is taken at its face value it would give the year 581 B.C., i.e. five years after the fall of Jerusalem in 586. There are, however, cogent reasons why the book should be dated some six centuries later than this. In the first place, there is no record that Baruch was ever in Babylon; according to Jer. 43:6, 7 he went to Egypt with Jeremiah. His name would, nevertheless, be a suitable pseudonym for a document purporting to come from the first years of the Babylonian Exile because of the prominent part he, with Jeremiah, played in those years. A similar historical error to that of Dan. 5:2 is made, namely that of making Belshazzar the son of Nebuchadnezzar whereas he was the son of Nabu-naid. It is possible that this error is dependent on Daniel because there is also a literary dependence, the prayer of confession in 1: 15 – 2: 19, esp. 2: 8–19, being parallel to Dan. 9: 4–19.

There are three other previous authors with whose work parts of Baruch shows strong affinity: first, 1: 15 – 3: 8 is clearly the work of one who was steeped in Jeremiah's writings; second, 4: 5 – 5: 9 has very strong affinities with the work of Deutero-Isaiah; and third, 5: 5–9 (or even 4: 36 – 5: 9) closely echoes the phrasing of Psalms of Solomon 11: 2–7. The latest of these authors is, of course, the author of Ps. Sol. 11 which, with the other psalms in that collection, is usually assigned to the time of Pompey's capture of Jerusalem in 63 B.C. If, therefore, the book of Baruch is later than all these we must look for a date later than Pompey and the most likely one will be that of the Roman War of A.D. 66–70. As we have seen[1] Babylon came to represent Rome in writings of the period, and it will not be difficult to see an allusion to Vespasian and his son Titus in the mention of Nebuchadnezzar and his son Belshazzar. Moreover, it would not be quite out of the question for Jews in A.D. 70 to recommend submission to their conquerors (2: 21 f.) although it would be difficult to imagine it being done in Maccabean times. The siege of Jerusalem would adequately account for the fearful sufferings of the Jews depicted in 2: 3, 24, and it was followed by destruction by fire 1: 2, 2: 26. The only difficulty about so late a date is the complete absence of any hope of resurrection, indeed 2: 17 implies that no such hope was ever in the author's knowledge.

Although it cannot be described as an apocalypse it has

[1] See p. 27.

some of the traits of apocalyptic, notably the pseudonymity of the author and the allusion to Rome and its rulers
by the mention of Babylon and its kings. The first two
parts were probably written in Hebrew and subsequently
translated into Greek. It is not certain what language the
third part was first written in; it may have been Greek,
but this turns on whether the dependence on the Greek of
Ps. Sol. can be proved to be original; if not, then that part
too may have been written in Hebrew originally.

CHAPTER X

THE LETTER OF JEREMIAH[1]

This chapter is a demonstration of the helplessness of idols
and the futility of their worship. It purports to have been
written by Jeremiah to the exiles in Babylon telling them
that they may have to remain there for anything up to
seven generations and that they must not be attracted to
the worship of idols (1-7). The idols are made by craftsmen,
but cannot speak; they are decked out with jewels as if
they were girls with a passion for jewellery, but the priests
steal their gold and silver to use for themselves, even to
spend on harlots. Their clothes rot, their faces get dirty
and their sceptre and dagger are useless, so why fear them?
(8-16). Their eyes get full of dust, their faces black with
dirt; birds, bats and cats make free on their bodies, and
the priests not only light many lamps, ignoring their
sightlessness, but even lock them in at night because they
cannot look after themselves (17-23). They have to be
cleaned of corrosion, to be carried about on men's backs
and to suffer the reproach of having their sacrifices misused even by the priests and their wives (24-29). They
stand there dumb while women make meals for them, and
the priests wail and howl before them, but then clothe
their women and children with clothes taken from the idols.
They cannot do any of the humane things that even a man

[1] R.S.V. In R.V. and A.V. it is headed The Epistle of Jeremy, and
printed as chapter 6 of the book of Baruch.

might do, let alone a god; they are like stones from the
mountain-side (30–40a). There these dumb creatures stand
while men pray to them to restore speech to a dumb man,
and the prostitutes ply their trade in the temple corridors
(40b–44). They are made of wood and stone, and if calamity comes the priests hide them for safety (45–52). They
cannot make kings, or determine the weather, or deliver
those who are wronged. If the temple were to catch fire
they would burn with it (53–56). They cannot save themselves from robbers; in fact, it would be better to be a king
with courage, or a kitchen pan doing its proper job; the
door of a house is better protection for the house than one
of these gods (57–59). God sends sun, moon and stars,
lightning and fire, on their errands—but what of these useless idols? (60–65). They cannot curse or bless; they cannot
control the elements; even the wild beasts are in better
case, for they can protect themselves (66–69). In short,
they are no better than scarecrows with rotting clothes
flecked by bird lime (70–73).

In brief, this is a scathing denunciation of idol worship,
so characteristic of Babylon, by a Babylonian Jew writing
pseudonymously in the name of Jeremiah. It would be well
known that Jeremiah did write a letter to the exiles (Jer.
29) and also that he did write a scornful attack on idols
(Jer. 10: 1–16). The author of this 'letter' knew the latter
passage and echoed verse 5 in verse 70 of the letter. He
also wrote in the tradition of Deutero-Isaiah especially as
found in 44: 9–20. That he wrote in Babylon is fairly certain because of his references to sacred processions (4, 26)
and to cultic prostitution (43). It is not possible to assess
the date at all closely. The dependence on Jeremiah and
Deutero-Isaiah implies a date after the Exile. The reference to a possible stay in Babylon of seven generations

G

suggests that upwards of 250 years have passed (if we reckon between thirty and forty years for a generation) since the fall of Jerusalem, thus bringing us to the end of the fourth century B.C. The only other possible clue to the date is the reference in 2 Macc. 2: 2 to gold and silver idols and their adornment, which could be taken to imply knowledge of the letter, but in fact it need not imply more than an acquaintance with Jer. 10: 1–16.

Although it is called a letter, its method of handling its theme is more suitable to utterance. The author drives home his points by reiteration, much as Deutero-Isaiah does. 'They are not gods, so do not fear them' is repeated in 16, 23, 29, 65 and 69. Three times the question is repeated: 'Why then must anyone think that they are gods, or call them gods?' (40, 44, 56).

In most Greek MSS the letter is placed after Lamentations, the order being Jeremiah, Baruch, Lamentations, Epistle of Jeremiah. In the Vulgate, as in some Greek MSS, it follows Baruch without a break, as it does in R.V. and A.V. Its Greek idiom is that of a translation; it has several awkward turns of phrase which can sometimes be eased by reconstructing a tentative Hebrew original. It was probably written in Hebrew in the first place.

CHAPTER XI

ADDITIONS TO THE BOOK OF DANIEL

In the Greek versions of Daniel there are three additions to the Hebrew text which have found their way into the Apocrypha as did the additions to the book of Esther. The additions are known as:

(i) The Prayer of Azariah and the Song of the Three Young Men.[1]
(ii) Susanna.[2]
(iii) Bel and the Dragon.[3]

Contents

(i) *The Prayer of Azariah and the Song of the Three Young Men*

Azariah prayed out of the fire in the furnace acknowledging that God had brought the Jews into affliction justly because they had failed in their loyalty to him. He begged God for mercy for the sake of Abraham to whom and through whom the promises had been made; he made humble submission to God and prayed that the enemy might be brought to disaster and thus to come to know God's power (1–22). The Chaldeans made the furnace even

---

[1] In A.V. and R.V. it is called: The Song of the Three Holy Children.
[2] In A.V. and R.V. it is called: The History of Susanna.
[3] So R.V. and R.S.V. In A.V. it is headed: The History of the Destruction of Bel and the Dragon, cut off from the end of Daniel. It contains, in fact, two separate stories.

hotter, but the three men were joined by the angel of the Lord and they sang their hymn of praise (23–28). The hymn calls upon all God's creatures to praise him, ending up with specific mention of Hananiah, Azariah and Mishael whom God delivered from the furnace (28–68).

(ii) *Susanna*

Susanna was a beautiful woman, admired by all, and especially by two elders who used to come to her husband Joakim's house on judicial business. They lusted after her and laid a plot either to possess her or to injure her maliciously. One day in the garden as she was about to bathe they pursued their plan. She had sent her maids indoors, so they revealed themselves to her and invited her to lie with them, or otherwise they would falsely malign her and declare that a young man had been with her and for that reason she had sent away her maids. She refused and summoned help. The elders persisted in their accusation and brought her to trial, where, by their false tales, they succeeded in having her convicted. But as they were leaving, Daniel declared that it was all wrong and that the men had given false witness. A fresh trial was held in which the men were asked, independently, under which tree the affair had taken place: one said a mastic tree and the other an evergreen oak. In this way, by their disagreement, they proved their falsehood and were condemned to death.

(iii) *Bel and the Dragon*

(a) *Bel*. Cyrus worshipped the god Bel, but Daniel, 'a companion of the king, and . . . the most honoured of his friends', worshipped his own God. Bel's daily allowance of food, which Cyrus believed to be eaten by the god, was twelve bushels of fine flour, forty sheep and fifty gallons of wine. Daniel challenged this belief, so he and the king put it to test by sealing the sanctuary. Daniel strewed the floor with ashes. In the morning the seal was intact but the food was gone. Then Daniel showed the king the footmarks in the ashes and it was then discovered that the priests and their families had a private entrance under the table and regularly ate the food.

(b) *The Dragon.* The Babylonians worshipped a dragon whose divinity was challenged by Daniel. He was allowed to prove his point, which he did by feeding the dragon on pitch, fat and hair boiled together to make cakes. 'The dragon ate them, and burst open.' The Babylonians were indignant with Daniel for so exposing their worship and they demanded punishment. He was thrown into a lions' den, but God kept him safe and had him miraculously fed by the prophet Habakkuk. At the end of seven days Daniel was found still alive and whole and the men who had caused him to be thrown there were themselves thrown in and eaten by the lions.

Unlike the Esther additions, which were written for the purpose of enlarging the book, these Daniel additions were probably in circulation independently, perhaps in Hebrew or Aramaic, and seemed to an editor to be suitable for inclusion with the Daniel story. Like the canonical book of Daniel, the additions exist in two forms, that of the Septuagint and that of Theodotion.[1] There are some differences between them and it is the latter version that has been translated in our English Bibles. In both versions the Prayer of Azariah and the Song of the Three Young Men

[1] Theodotion made a revision of the LXX some time in the second half of the second century A.D., and for some reason his version of Daniel superseded that of the Septuagint.

occur between verses 23 and 24 of Daniel 3, and Bel and the Dragon stand at the end of the book. In Theodotion Susanna stands at the head of the book and in LXX it stands between Daniel 12 and Bel and the Dragon. The contents are not an integral part of the book although an editor thought they might fit. That is why in both versions Susanna was placed outside the book; the editor who put it at the beginning possibly thought it might refer to Daniel in his early days before the period of the book that bears his name. The contents of the prayer of Azariah are not applicable to his condition. The editor doubtless found the Prayer and the Song, liked them and worked them into Daniel at 3: 23 by adding a prose introduction to the Prayer and the Song. He probably also added verse 66, thus adapting the Song to its new position. It is not possible to say when the insertion was made, whether in the original Hebrew–Aramaic form of the book or in the Greek; slightly in favour of the former is the fact that Dan. 3: 24 offers no reason for the king's astonishment. Some statement about what caused it may have fallen out or been displaced, when the Prayer and Song were inserted. Such an early insertion, coupled with the complete disappearance of such a statement, would suggest that the book of Daniel with its additions was so popular that when it was desired to re-introduce it in its original shorter form that had to be done by removing the additions from one of the current copies.

The Prayer of Azariah is a fine expression of contrition and supplication for God's mercy, but it is entirely inapplicable to the immediate circumstances of the men in the furnace. In effect it is a psalm of lamentation for the community. The mention of the loss of prince, prophet, leader and all kinds of sacrifices (15) shows it to belong, almost beyond doubt, to the dark days of the Maccabaean rising. Josephus, in telling the story of the three men in the furnace (Ant. X. x. 5), shows no knowledge of either the Prayer or the Song. This probably means that in his day the copies normally used in the Jewish church had no additions. On the other hand, the Prayer and the Song were both popular pieces and ultimately came to be included in the collection of hymns in the Septuagint known as the Odes and used in Christian worship. Ode 9 is headed The Prayer of Azariah, and Ode 10 either The Hymn of our Fathers (Codex Alexandrinus) or The Hymn of the Three Young Men (Codex Turocensis). It is the second of these that is followed in our English versions.

The Song of the Three Young Men is familiar to many because verses 35–65 are very similar to Ps. 148 and are also found in the Prayer Book as the Benedicite. Verses 67 f. are reminiscent of Ps. 136: 1 f.

The story of Susanna may at one time have been a favourite tale in secular circles. If so it appealed to an editor who possessed that genius for religion which the Jews so persistently showed and who incorporated it in the book of Daniel and re-inspired it with the ethical strength of Yahwism. The Septuagint version gives it no geographical setting, whereas Theodotion places it in Babylon. It has also been suggested that the introduction of Daniel's name was due to Theodotion and that the original form of the LXX version had only an anonymous young man. If the Babylonian setting is entirely due to Theodotion, then the original story mentioned no geographical situation and could have been placed anywhere in the imagination of the reader. The story comprises two familiar motifs, that of a woman falsely accused and that of a wise young judge. Daniel's wisdom was proverbial, Ezek. 28: 3, and it is also worth recording that the Danel (possibly a variant form of Daniel) of the Ugaritic texts was known as one who protected widows and orphans.[1]

The original language of the story is in some dispute. Most scholars think it probably had a Hebrew original, although they readily acknowledge the fact that two puns which occur in the Greek version (54, 55, 58, 59) cannot have been translated. If there was a Semitic original there may have been puns within that language, in which case the translator cleverly invented fresh ones, or the translator may have developed the original at this point where he saw an opportunity of punning. The puns in question are based on the names of the trees: mastic—*schinon* suggested *schisei* shall cut, and evergreen oak—*prinon* suggested *prisai* to saw.

Bel and the Dragon is in two parts. The one deals with the unmasking of the idol Bel, and the other with proving that the dragon was no god. The dragon may be associated with the primaeval monster *tiamat* whom Marduk had to subdue before he could create the world: but in all probability it was not a monster at all but a living snake or serpent. Such creatures are known to have been worshipped in some parts of the ancient near east.

The strewing of the ashes over the floor to discover footprints is a familiar device in fairy tales. The inclusion of Habakkuk in the story is evidence of the popularity of the prophet Habakkuk and probably of the book that bears his name, as also is the fact that a commentary on the book was discovered among the documents at Qumrân. The Septuagint adds a superscription which runs: 'From a prophecy of Ambakum [= Habakkuk] son of Jesus, of the

[1] G. R. Driver, *Canaanite Myths and Legends*, 1956, p. 53 (Aqhat II. v. 7).

tribe of Levi'. The feeding of Daniel while he was still in the lions' den by Habakkuk, may be derived from a popular tale about the prophet.

The story almost certainly existed originally in a Semitic language.

CHAPTER XII

THE PRAYER OF MANASSEH[1]

THIS short prayer of fifteen verses is a simple straightforward confession of sin and prayer for forgiveness from God who has 'appointed repentance for me, who am a sinner'.

The second book of Chronicles adds to the story of king Manasseh (as told in II Kings 21: 1-18) an account of how he was taken to Babylon as a captive. While he was there he humbled himself before God and asked God for favour. He was restored to his throne and from that time on was a model king (II Chron. 33: 10-13). The Chronicler's summary of his reign has these words: 'Now the rest of the acts of Manasseh, and his prayer to his God . . . are in the Chronicles of the Kings of Israel. And his prayer, and how God received his entreaty . . . are written in the Chronicles of the Seers' (II Chron. 33: 18 f.). What we have in the prayer, apparently, is an editor's reconstruction of what Manasseh was likely to have said as he prayed to God in his distress. We may compare it, therefore, with the additions to Esther and Daniel. In the E addition to Esther we find a prayer of Mordecai and a prayer of Esther, and in the Daniel additions a prayer of Azariah and The Song of the Three Young Men.

Nothing is known of its date or of the circumstances of

[1] So R.S.V. A.V. and R.V. have this title: The Prayer of Manasses King of Judah, when he was holden captive in Babylon.

its composition. It is possible that the first attempt to translate the books of Chronicles into Greek was more of a targumic paraphrase than a literal rendering and that the prayer was a part of that paraphrase. No trace of such a paraphrase of Chronicles remains, however. The earliest positive date at which the prayer is known is the publication of an early Christian writing, possibly second century, known as the Didascalia. The book illustrates God's mercy towards repentant sinners and instances David, Jonah, Hezekiah and Manasseh.

The prayer evidently won a place in Christian usage and worship and was included among the fourteen 'Odes' or canticles which followed the Psalms in Codex A (early fifth century). The Odes was a collection of songs, mainly Biblical, such as that in Exod. 15, and included the Magnificat, the Nunc Dimittis and the Benedictus. The prayer appears as No. 8 and is headed 'Prayer of Manasseh'. It is the title alone, however, that associates it with Manasseh. There is no personal reference at all in the prayer that would associate it with king Manasseh rather than any other person. But the title is constant enough in the manuscripts and is doubtless original. That is to say, the prayer was composed to serve the purpose indicated by its present title, but by whom and at what time it was composed cannot be said.

It was probably written originally in Greek for there is no phrase in it that demands a Hebrew form underlying the Greek. It well deserves its place in the Apocrypha for the sincerity of its thought and the purity of its worship of God.

CHAPTER XIII

I MACCABEES[1]

CONTENTS

1: 1–64. Introductory events: describing the advent of
Antiochus Epiphanes over the Seleucid Empire,[2] the introduction of Greek customs among the Jews, the subsequent
prohibition of Jewish worship and practices, and the setting up of the 'abomination that makes desolate'.[3] Many
chose death rather than conform.

2: 1–70. Mattathias. After a genealogy of Mattathias and
a dirge over Jerusalem (1–14), the chapter goes on to describe the stand against Greek worship and sacrifice at
Modein (15–28) and then the massacre of a thousand Jews
who had fled to the hills and would not fight on the Sabbath day (29–38). To avoid further bloodshed the decision
is taken to fight on the Sabbath if need be, and Mattathias
and his followers begin to take the offensive. They are
joined by the Hasideans (39–48). At his death Mattathias
appoints Judas as captain, specially commended Simon
and exhorted his sons to hold firm to their cause (49–70).

3: 1 – 9: 22. Judas Maccabeus.

*3: 1 – 4: 61. The early stages of the revolt up to the re-
dedication of the Temple.*[4] An ode in honour of Judas (3: 1–

---

[1] In A.V. and R.V. The First Book of the Maccabees.
[2] The date given for this is according to Seleucid reckoning, i.e.
beginning at 312 B.C. when Seleucus I assumed sovereignty.
[3] Twenty-fifth Chislev, 168. 1: 54 wrongly has fifteenth.
[4] Twenty-fifth Chislev, 165.

9). Judas gains some initial successes (3: 10–26). The
Syrians prepare on a large scale under Lysias, who sends
Nicanor and Gorgias into Judaea (3: 27–60). Georgias is
defeated by Judas at Emmaus (4: 1–25), and then Lysias,
provoked by the defeat which was so contrary to the king's
wishes, himself enters the field and suffers defeat at
Bethzur; he retires to Antioch to reassemble his army
(4: 26–35). Judas takes advantage of the lull in fighting to
enter Jerusalem and re-dedicate the Temple. This takes
place on 25th Chislev on the anniversary, three years later,
of the desecration (4: 36–59). He fortifies the Temple
mount and Bethzur (4: 60, 61).

5: 1 – 7: 50; the fighting continues: resentment is shown
against the Jews by Edomites, Ammonites and Baenites
but their attacks are repulsed (5: 1–8). Simon successfully
wages further battles in Galilee and Judas in Gilead. Continued fighting in Judaea was not successful because it had
not been authorized by Judas (5: 9–68). Antiochus IV dies
and is succeeded by Antiochus V, Eupator (6: 1–17).
Fighting then centres on the citadel at Jerusalem, whose
garrison constantly harass the Jews in the city, and in
the fortress of Bethzur. Judas is not successful in these
battles. Eleazar is killed at Bethzur (6: 18–54). Difficulties elsewhere now claim the attention of the Seleucid
leaders and a peace is patched up between Lysias
and Judas (6: 55–63). Demetrius I succeeds Antiochus
V, who, with Lysias, is put to death. Bacchides and
Alcimus go to Judaea and are welcomed by the Hasideans
but betray the trust put in them (7: 1–20). Alcimus is re-
instated as high-priest, but the successes of Judas cause
him to appeal to Syria. Nicanor is sent but is defeated
(7: 21–50).

8: 1 – 9: 22; last months of Judas' leadership. A treaty of non-aggression and mutual help is made with Rome (8: 1–32). Judas is killed at the battle of Berea[1] (9: 1–22).

9: 23 – 12: 53. Jonathan's leadership. 160–143 B.C. While Bacchides attempts to establish some authority among the pro-hellenistic Jews, Jonathan Maccabeus is elected to succeed Judas by the resisting movement (9: 23–31). Jonathan's brother John is killed while on a mission to the Nabateans to seek shelter among them. Jonathan avenges his death (9: 32–49). Bacchides consolidates his position in Palestine, but returns to Antioch on the death of Alcimus (9: 50–57). He is soon recalled to Judaea, where he is defeated by Jonathan at Bethbasi; there followed peace for five years (9: 58–73). During a disputed succession to the Seleucid throne, Jonathan's aid is enlisted by both sides in turn, by Demetrius (10: 1–14), by Alexander Balas who appointed him high-priest (152) (10: 15–21) and by Demetrius again (10: 22–47). After the death of Demetrius, Alexander further honours Jonathan, making him general and Governor of Judaea; in this capacity Jonathan defeats Apollonius who supported the claims of Demetrius II (146) (10: 48–89). The claim of Demetrius II is also successfully supported by Ptolemy VI at whose instigation Alexander loses his life. Jonathan wins the favour of Demetrius II (11: 1–37). When Trypho, a Syrian general, produces a son of Alexander,[2] Jonathan for a time remains loyal to Demetrius II and helps him to repulse Trypho (11: 38–53), then when Trypho and Antiochus renew their claims and promise Jonathan renewal of his governorship and the appointment of Simon to control the sea-board strip (the Paralia) Jonathan transfers his support (11: 54–74). The treaty with Rome is renewed and negotiations with Sparta

---

[1] Possibly to be identified with Bereth, ten miles north of Jerusalem.
[2] Who became Antiochus VI, 146–142.

begun (12: 1–23). Jonathan continues to strengthen his
military position in support of Trypho but is captured by
trickery (12: 24–53) (and ultimately killed (13: 23)).

13: 1 – 16: 24. Simon Maccabeus. 143–134 B.C. Simon
succeeds Jonathan: Trypho has Jonathan put to death,
then on being forced to withdraw from Palestine he kills
Antiochus VI. Demetrius II makes a treaty with Simon
(13: 1–42). Simon captures Gazara and the citadel in Jerusalem and appoints his son John Hyrcanus as commander-
in-chief (13: 43–53). Demetrius is captured by the Par-
thians (14: 1–3). Here there is a eulogy on Simon (14: 4–
15). Alliance with Rome and Sparta is renewed (14: 16–
24). A decree is made in honour of Simon confirming in
him the hereditary high-priesthood (14: 25–49). A further
claimant to the Seleucid throne comes forward, Antiochus
VII, Sidetes;[1] he enlists Simon's support by the offer of
the right to coin money in his own name (15: 1–9). Antiochus besieges Trypho in Dor (15: 10–14). Envoys come to
the east from Rome bringing pro-Jewish decrees (15: 15–
24). Antiochus repudiates his pact with Simon and sends
Cendebaus to harrass the Jews (15: 25–41). Cendebaus is
defeated by Simon's sons Judas and John (16: 1–10).
Ptolemy, an officer in the army, plots against Simon and
his sons, killing Simon, Judas and Mattathias. John es-
capes slaughter and becomes Simon's successor (16: 11–24).

I Maccabees may be described as a history of the Maccabean revolt. It opens with an account of the reasons for
revolt and ends with the death of the last of the five
brothers, Simon, in 134 B.C. Their successors, beginning
with Simon's son John Hyrcanus, came to be known as the
Hasmoneans after Hasmon, who, according to Josephus,

[1] Named after Side in Pamphilia to which place he was evacuated.

was the great-grandfather of Mattathias. The book is
therefore rightly called the book of the Maccabees and at
the end there is a brief mention of the fact that the acts
and achievements of John Hyrcanus are 'written in the
chronicles of his high-priesthood, from the time that he
became high priest after his father'.[1] Unless they are to be
regarded as an editorial addition, these last verses might imply that the author of I Maccabees lived after, or towards
the end of, the reign of John Hyrcanus (134–105 B.C.).

We know nothing more of the author than the little that
can be gleaned from the book itself. He appears to have
had a Sadducean outlook; there is no hint of a belief in
resurrection although the record of the last days of Mattathias (2: 49 ff.) would have been enriched by such a belief.
Apparently he was not so insistent on strict sabbath observance as a Pharisee might have shown himself; he was
tolerant towards those who felt constrained to break sabbath rules in the interests of the revolt, 2: 41, 9: 43 ff. The
reference to the part played by the Hasideans (2: 42, 7:
1–20) could have been written equally well by either a
Sadducee or a Pharisee, but the objectivity of it suggests
the former. He speaks well of the high-priest throughout
the book (5: 62, 13: 3, 14: 25, 16: 2). Josephus does not
mention the book, but his story of the period is clearly
based on I Maccabees, supplemented from Greek sources,
until I Macc. 13: 42 is reached and then he seems to leave
I Maccabees and to rely on his Greek sources. There is no
obvious reason why Josephus should have discontinued
his use of I Macc. just at this point, i.e. the death of Antiochus and the recognition of Simon's kingship. It is just

---

[1] It is tempting to regard this reference as pointing to the beginning
of a history of the Hasmoneans comparable with this of the Maccabees.
If there were such, no trace now remains.

possible that the book originally finished at that point with the words: 'And the people began to write in their documents and contracts, "In the first year of Simon the great high priest and commander and leader of the Jews"'. But there is no evidence to support this. At least we may say that Josephus put his faith in I Maccabees, with the possible exception of the last three chapters, as a reliable historical document.

Can we follow Josephus in this and accept I Maccabees as trustworthy? In so far as any ancient historian may be trusted, the author of I Maccabees may be. To the best of his knowledge, the author gave what he believed to be the true sequence of events and in the speeches and documents, in the manner of ancient historians, he gave what he thought were the appropriate words. There is no reason to think that he was very far wrong about their general import. He does not appear to have had any axe to grind and there is no distortion of fact in the interest of theory.

He doubtless drew his material from a number of different sources. Some of it may have come from eye-witnesses to whom the vivid intimacy of detail in a number of places may be due (cf. 6: 39, 7: 33, 9: 39). The author himself may have witnessed some of the later events.

There are several poems in the book, namely:

> 1: 24–28: a dirge for Judaea
> 1: 36–40: a dirge for Jerusalem
> 2: 7–13: Mattathias' lament for Jerusalem
> 3: 3–9: in praise of Judas
> 3: 45: a dirge for Jerusalem
> 14: 4–15: in praise of Simon.

It could be claimed that these were composed at the time to which they refer and had become part and parcel of the

H

oral tradition of the period. If this were so, the author of
I Macc. may have been the first to commit them to writing.
But it is equally possible to claim that the author himself
composed them. One thing they have in common is a dependence on the Old Testament for words and phrases.
The poems therefore are not of serious concern in consider-
ing what written material lay before the author as he com-
menced his story. Other passages, however, suggest that
there were written documents from which he could quote.
The letter to Jonathan (11: 30–37) ends with the words
'take care to make a copy of this,[1] and let it be given to
Jonathan and put up in a conspicuous place on the holy
mountain'. In 14: 18, 27 we read of bronze tablets written
by the Romans to Simon and of other bronze tablets 'upon
pillars on mount Zion' written by the Jews to honour
Simon and his family. A decree concerning Simon was
written on bronze tablets and copies were deposited in 'a
conspicuous place in the precincts of the sanctuary', 14:
48 f. The words of a Roman document pledging mutual
help are given in 8: 23–32 and are said to be a copy of the
letter which they wrote 'on bronze tablets, and sent to
Jerusalem to remain with them there as a memorial of
peace and alliance'. The discovery of two copper rolls
(originally parts of one roll) at Qumrân affords evidence of
the use of metal for documents in the first century A.D.[2]
These references to depositing documents in Jerusalem or
affixing them there in a conspicuous place shows that the
author knew of the existence of documents, but whether or
not he used them and quoted verbatim cannot be proved.
It is clear that he intended the words to be taken as exact

---

[1] A letter from Demetrius to Lasthenes, incorporated in the letter to
Jonathan.

[2] *Biblical Archaeologist*, XIX, 1956, No. 3, pp. 61 ff.

quotation. On the other hand, ancient authors were accustomed to give their own reconstruction of what would have been said or written. Most of the documents cited are diplomatic documents (10: 18–20, 25–45, 11: 30–37, 12: 6–18, 20–23, 14: 20–23, 15: 2–9, 16–21), the others being a letter from Gilead appealing for help against the 'Gentiles', 5: 10–13, a panegyric on Simon, 14: 27–45 and the terms of a treaty of alliance between the Romans and the Jews, 8: 23–32. In the nature of the case some of these would be given permanent record, though we do not know how far they would be accessible to the historian.

Such a lively consciousness of the existence of written records, together with the explicit reference to the Chronicles of the priesthood of John Hyrcanus (16: 24), belongs to an author with a true conscience in historical writing, and we may, for want of more positive evidence, regard I Maccabees as a reliable record.

There remains to mention one other literary dependence which is apparent again and again in the book, namely, on the books of the Old Testament. First it may be remarked that the author implies that prophecy had for the time being ceased to be, but that if a prophet were to arise his word would be authoritative (4: 46, 9: 27, 14: 41). He sees in the attempt to break down the wall of the inner court of the Temple a tearing down of the work of the prophets (9: 54) presumably because the prophets emphasized the need to avoid being caught up by the idolatry that was rife among the Gentiles. This reverence for the works of the prophets stands second to that for the 'Books of the law' or the 'Book of the covenant' (1: 56 f.) and shows that there was already a lively sense of sacred scripture. It is difficult to say what was the extent of the scripture which was recognized at that time. Some indication may perhaps

be seen in I Macc. 2: 52–60, where there is a short review
of leading men of the Old Testament. It begins with Abraham and ends with Daniel and his three companions. One
may suppose that *Daniel* had already been recognized as
one of the sacred writings, although it must have been a
very recent addition to them and presumably added at the
end. The term 'abomination of desolation'[1] (1: 54) is used
in *Daniel* (11: 31, 12: 11) and may have been taken from
that book. Allusions to the Old Testament are found in 3:
45, and 14: 6–15; the refrain of Ps. 118 and 136 occurs at
4: 24 and Ps. 79: 2 f. is found in a shortened form in 7: 17.
I Macc. 4: 30–33 alludes to the exploits of David and
Jonathan against the Philistines, while 5: 48 echoes Num.
20: 17, 21: 22 and 7: 37 seems dependent on I Kings 8: 38–
43. Apart from the inclusion of Daniel this agrees with
what is implied by ben Sira's list of famous men and is
made explicit in the prologue to the translation of ben
Sira's book which speaks of the 'law, the prophets and the
other books of our fathers' as a clearly recognized corpus of
sacred scripture.

One wonders whether I Maccabees might have been included in the Jewish Canon if the canonical histories—
Judges, Samuel and Kings—had not been included among
the 'Prophets' and thus, since prophetic inspiration had
ceased, precluded from further additions.

There is no clear indication of the date of writing. If the
author intended only to write of the Maccabees and deliberately excluded the Hasmoneans the story could have
been written at almost any time, although the favourable
attitude towards the Romans would be easier to understand before 63 B.C., when Pompey captured Jerusalem,
than after it. But the exclusion of the Hasmoneans may be

[1] R.S.V. translated the phrase as 'desolating sacrilege'.

because the author was writing during the reign of John Hyrcanus (134–105 B.C.) and thus was not in a position to go further. The last two verses of the book refer to the acts of John being found written in the chronicles of his priesthood, and if these verses were original they suggest that the author lived during that reign and wrote towards the end of it or immediately afterwards.

ORIGINAL LANGUAGE

The book was almost certainly written in Hebrew (or Aramaic), but no trace of a Semitic original is extant; we are dependent on the Greek translation for our text. Apart from several instances of the retention of Hebrew idiom in the Greek (cf. 1: 9, 1: 12) there are two[1] pieces of evidence in favour of a Hebrew original. (i) Origen[2] gave the book the name *Sarbeth Sabanaiel* [Σαρβηθ Σαβαναιελ] whose meaning is not yet fully understood but which looks like a Hebrew phrase meaning 'prince (or book[3]) of the house of Sabaniel'. Some evidence to link Sabaniel in some way with either Maccabee or Hasmon would be useful. (ii) In 14: 28 we read 'which is the third year of Simon the great high priest, in Asaramel, in the great assembly of the priests and the people . . .' The word Asaramel seems to be a trans-literation of the Hebrew for 'court of the people of God'.

It would indeed be only natural that such a story, concerned with the struggle of the Jewish people for religious freedom and the right to read their Book of the law and to practise their own form of worship, would be written in the native tongue.

---

[1] Or three if we accept the evidence of mistranslation of the Hebrew in 6: 34, which should surely be translated 'They made the elephants drunk with the juice of grapes'.

[2] Mentioned by Eusebius, *Hist. Eccles*, vi. 25. 2.

[3] Taking *sar* to be a contraction of *sepher*.

CHAPTER XIV

II MACCABEES

SUMMARY OF CONTENTS

I. Two letters from Judaea to Egypt concerning the festival of Purification[1] (1: 1–2: 18)

(1) 1: 1–10a dated 124 B.C. and written to remind the Egyptian Jews about keeping the festival.

(2) 1: 10b – 2: 18 another letter urging the Egyptian community to keep the festival, but the letter is undated and may possibly refer to the first celebration, at the actual re-dedication of the Temple in 165 B.C. Within this letter there is a digression (1: 18b – 2: 15) giving two traditions concerning the altar fire: (i) that Nehemiah sent a mission to recover the fire that had been hidden away by priests at the fall of Jerusalem (1: 18b–36); (ii) that the fire was removed at Jeremiah's instigation; he himself hid away the tabernacle, the ark and the altar of incense (2: 1–15).

II. Preface to the history (2: 19–32)

This says that what follows is an epitome of the history, written in five books, by Jason of Cyrene.

---

[1] In 1: 9 it is called 'the feast of booths in the month of Chislev'. The proper month for the feast of booths was Tishri, but II Macc. 10: 6 f. says that the festival of Purification was celebrated on similar lines to that of booths. This may have been because the community had been in hiding and had not properly celebrated the feast of booths that was due shortly before the re-dedication. It was a festival of great rejoicing, cf. I Macc. 4: 56 ff. Josephus called it the 'Feast of Lights' because the lighting of lamps and candles played a large part in its celebration.

III. Jewish intrigues as the causes of the troubles (3: 1 – 4: 50)

Seleucus and Heliodorus are frustrated in their attempt, at the instigation of Simon (a Tobiad), to raid the Temple treasury and take the monies deposited there for safe-keeping (3: 1–40). Simon slanders the high priest Onias whose brother Jason, by ingratiating himself with Antiochus Epiphanes after his accession, is appointed high-priest. Jason then begins to encourage Greek practices in Jerusalem (4: 1–22). Menelaus, brother of Simon, is sent on a mission to Antiochus by Jason, but when he comes to the king he outbids Jason for the high-priesthood. He secures the death of Onias and maintains his power in face of great unpopularity (4: 23–50).

IV. The enforced Hellenization of Judaea (5: 1 – 7 : 42)

An apparition of a heavenly army over Jerusalem forebodes disaster (5: 1–4). Antiochus in Egypt hears of Jason's resumption of the high-priesthood following a report of the death of Antiochus. He takes this to be a sign of revolt and on his return he enters Jerusalem pillaging and profaning. Menelaus is restored to office and Judas Maccabeus flees to the hills to escape the indiscriminate slaughter that follows (5: 5–27). Hellenization by force is attempted; several martyrdoms take place, two women for circumcising their children, Eleazar, at the age of ninety, for refusing to eat swine's flesh, and seven brothers and their mother (6: 1 – 7: 42).

V. Judas leads the revolt

The story is carried as far as the death of Nicanor (8: 1 – 15: 36). Judas leads the revolt and divides the rebel army into four in charge of each of his brothers. One brother, Eleazar, is appointed to read from scripture, and

his name, meaning *God's help*, is made a watchword (8:
1–36). Death of Antiochus; on his death-bed he is said to
have been seized by contrition over his treatment of the
Jews and to have had a letter of greeting and clemency
sent to them (9: 1–29). The Temple is captured by Judas
and purified (10: 1–8). Further successful campaigns of
Judas are described, despite signs of treachery shown by
some of his leaders (10: 9–38). Lysias, the Syrian general, is
defeated at Bethzur and four letters of peace are exchanged:
(i) from Lysias to the Jews; (ii) from Antiochus to Lysias;
(iii) from Antiochus to the Jewish people; and (iv) from the
two Roman ambassadors to the Jewish people (11: 1–38).
Further fighting takes place; against Joppa, in requital of
a trick played on the Jews by the people of that place, and
against the Syrians and the Hellenizers (12: 1–45). After
more fighting, Lysias and Antiochus V (Eupator) are
forced to come to terms with the Jews (13: 1–26). The
governorship of Nicanor; he and Judas form a friendship
which is broken by the treachery of Alcimus (14: 1–46).
Nicanor is defeated and killed by the Jews (15: 1–36).

VI. *Epilogue* (15: 37–39).

To pass from I Maccabees to II Maccabees is to move
into a very different atmosphere. It has been said that I
Maccabees is to II Maccabees as Samuel and Kings are to
Chronicles. One passes from a more or less objective writing of a historical narrative to a recital of certain events,
not all of which are recorded elsewhere and therefore not
all subject to verification, and which are told not so much
for their own sake as for what they illustrate and teach.
Throughout the book the author is concerned to show, as
the Chronicler does, that God's power is all-supreme and
may be brought to the aid of his servants provided they

ask in the right way at the right time. When God did inter-
vene in the affairs of his people it was in a miraculous way.
In his preface the author draws attention to the 'appearances which came from heaven to those who strove zealously on behalf of Judaism', but in his narrative he also
includes appearances of heavenly creatures to the enemies
of the Jews. Heliodorus, trying to pillage the Temple, was
struck helpless by a vision of a horseman and of two angels,
and was frustrated in his purpose (3: 22–30).

Immediately prior to Jason's rising there was a vision
over the city for forty days of golden-clad horsemen making mimic battle; it was taken as a good omen (5: 1–4).
When Judas faced Timotheus in battle he prayed for God's
help and was answered by a vision to the enemy of five
heavenly horsemen at the head of the Jewish forces (10:
29–31). When he faced Lysias he was encouraged by a
horseman in white, who appeared at the head of them
brandishing weapons of gold (11: 8). There is no record of
a vision on the occasion of Nicanor's defeat, but Judas did
encourage his men by telling them of a vision he himself
had had (15: 12–16), and as Nicanor and his men advanced
'Judas and his men met the enemy in battle with invoca-
tion to God and prayers. So, fighting with their hands and
praying to God in their hearts, they laid low no less than
thirty-five thousand men, and were greatly gladdened by
God's manifestation' (15: 26, 27). On the other hand, there
is no mention of heavenly intervention when Antiochus
attacked Jerusalem and profaned the Temple for 'if it had
not happened that they were involved in many sins, this
man would have been scourged and turned back from his
rash act as soon as he came forward, just as Heliodorus
was, whom Seleucus the king sent to inspect the treasury'
(5: 11–20).

This last passage is one of many places where the author either points a moral, or shows how vastly superior the Jews are to any other nation by reason of their faith in God and their devout practices. After describing the conduct of the people under Jason's encouragement and their almost complete abandonment to Hellenism he goes on to say that disaster overtook them, 'for it is no light thing to show irreverence to the divine laws—a fact which later events will make clear' (4: 17).[1] He states his purpose explicitly in 6: 12: 'Now I urge those who read this book not to be depressed by such calamities, but to recognize that these punishments were designed not to destroy but to discipline our people'. The sin with which he is concerned is that of apostasy.

In nearly every part of his narrative he shows his sympathies to be with the more pious party in Israel, those who came ultimately to be called Pharisees and whose chief concern was zeal for the law and its observance. It is no surprise therefore to find him expressing a hope in resurrection (7: 9, 14, 23, 36; 12: 43), in which respect the Pharisees differed from the Sadducees. It will be seen therefore that I and II Maccabees reflect these two widely differing parties in Judaism, the Sadducaean and the Pharisaic respectively. The Pharisaic sympathies shown by II Maccabees are to be seen in the several references to the observance of the sabbath (6: 11, 8: 25 ff., 12: 38, 15: 1 f.) and there is no reference to the decision to fight on the sabbath day in self protection (cf. I Macc. 2: 41). They are also to be seen in the way the author writes up details of the feud between the Tobiads and the Oniads; it is clearly written by an Oniad partisan (4: 1–6).

In some slight degree the book resembles the Old Testa-

[1] Cf. 4: 38; 5: 6, 10; 8: 23, 36; 9: 5; 11: 13; 12: 43–45; 13: 8.

ment book of Esther in focusing attention on two festivals, as the book of Esther does on one only, that of Purim. The two festivals are (i) that held to commemorate the re-dedication of the Temple and known as Chanukka, and (ii) that known as Nicanor's day, one of the days on which it was forbidden to fast (Meg. Taanith xii. 30). The celebration of the festival of Purification is the subject of the two letters with which the book opens. The greater part of the rest of the book virtually sets out the *raison d'être* of the festival, whose first celebration is described in 10: 1–7 and its permanent celebration decreed in verse 8. It is reported as beginning on the anniversary, the 25th day of Chislev, of the day on which Antiochus entered the Temple and defiled it. For the sheer joy expressed in it, the festival is comparable with the festival of booths or tabernacles which, according to II Macc. 10: 6, was the pattern for it. The very last verse of the book, apart from the short epilogue, tells of the decree to celebrate Nicanor's day (15: 36) and it is towards this that the final chapters of the book converge as they tell of the defeat and death of Nicanor.

The author's purpose in telling the story and the scope of it are set out in 2: 19–22. 'The story of Judas Maccabeus and his brothers, and the purification of the great temple, and the dedication of the altar, and further the wars against Antiochus Epiphanes and his son Eupator, and the appearances which came from heaven to those who strove zealously on behalf of Judaism, so that though few in number they seized the whole land and pursued the barbarian hordes, and recovered the temple famous throughout the world and freed the city and restored the laws that were about to be abolished, while the Lord with great kindness became gracious to them.' The order of events in

the story is different at some points from that given in
I Maccabees as will be seen from the following table:

I Maccabees	II Maccabees
Victory of Judas over Ly-sias, 4: 26–35	Death of Antiochus Epi-phanes, ch. 9
Dedication of Temple, 4: 36–51	Dedication of Temple, 10: 1–8
Fighting with neighbouring enemies, ch. 5	Victory over Lysias, 11: 1–15
Death of Antiochus Epi-phanes, 6: 1–17	Fighting against neigh-bours, ch. 12

The order of events followed by II Maccabees may have
been dictated by a desire to make the period of oppression
as short as possible and to show how the chief enemies of
the Jews were both defeated in a comparatively short time.
This is made all the more probable by the fact that in 10: 3
the period is given as lasting two years: 'They purified the
sanctuary, and they made another altar of sacrifice; then,
striking fire out of flint, they offered sacrifices after a lapse
of two years'. It is not clear whether this view of the order
of events was due to the epitomist's source, Jason of
Cyrene, or to the epitomist himself, or to a later editor who
added the two letters at the beginning, of which the second
clearly makes the celebration of the dedication festival
follow the death of Antiochus (1: 11–18).

The author (or epitomist) had other things in view besides that of giving a history of the Maccabean revolt. As
we have noted he wrote to explain the significance and importance of celebrating the two festivals, that which followed the death of Antiochus (in his view) and that which
followed the death of Nicanor. But equally clear is his

desire to enhance the prestige of the Jews, as far as he is able, by perpetuating legends such as that of the seven martyred brothers, sons of a brave woman. He tells in another place, with apparent relish, of the extremes of self-torture to which a pious Jew would submit (14: 37–46).

There is yet a further aim, a more significant one, namely, to extol God as sovereign Lord of the universe and as the protector of his chosen people. Although the author has much to say about the courage, skill and wisdom of the men who take part in the story, as, for instance, in the record of Judas' leadership in 15: 6–19, it is all subordinate to the will and power of God in heaven. It is to him that they turn for help in their hour of need; it is he who sends them help so often in a supernatural 'manifestation' and to whom they ascribe the victory when it is won. The disease-ridden Antiochus Epiphanes is made to declare that 'It is right to be subject to God, and no mortal should think that he is equal to God' (9: 12). Not only is God all-powerful, but he is utterly just. The author makes a point of showing, and indeed admitting, that when disaster befalls the Jews it is the result of their own lawless behaviour. For this reason no apparition is given to Antiochus when he desecrates the Temple because the Jews were too deeply involved in sin, and both they and their sanctuary must suffer the proper punishment (5: 17–20). Again, heavy losses among the ranks of the Jews are found to be due to secret apostasy on their part as revealed by the 'sacred tokens of the idols' that were found under the tunics of dead soldiers (12: 40).

This emphasis on the sovereign power of God and the justice of his dealings with men may well be the real reason for a second account of the Maccabean revolt alongside that given by I Maccabees. The author must have felt that he understood the full pattern of events and that it was worthy of publication. There is a distinct pattern in his order of events: the first celebration of the festival of Purification followed upon the death of the arch-oppressor Antiochus (ch. 9), since only after his death could full freedom be thought possible, and the book ends with the celebration of the death of the worst of the political and military enemies of the Jews, Nicanor. Part of the tracery of this pattern seems to be the shortening of the time of the oppression to two years (10: 3).[1]

II Maccabees covers the same period of history as I Maccabees 1–7, and it is conceivable that the author intended his narrative to displace I Maccabees because he thought his pattern of events was superior. If this was so we may suppose that II Maccabees was written a generation or two later than I Maccabees, although there is no clear evidence that its author knew or used the earlier book. The reference to John, father of Eupolemus, in 4: 11 might be thought to be an allusion to the paragraph about the mission to Rome in I Macc. 8: 17–32, although there the mission is carried out by the son and not the father. The author's main source was a five-volume history of the period by Jason of Cyrene which the author claims to have abridged (2: 23–32). If we accept what the author himself says, his method of abridgment was to omit dates and other chronological and statistical material and to concentrate on such passages as had homiletic and parenetic value. We know nothing at all of this five-volume history except the little that can be gleaned from II Maccabees. The following tentative division of the material between the five books may be offered for consideration:

[1] There is no need to suppose, as some do, that this is an error for three. The author plainly intended it, even if it was wishful thinking.

(1) The Oniads and Tobiads: Onias, Jason and Menelaus (3: 1 – 4: 50).

(2) Antiochus enters Jerusalem: Jewish martyrs
(5: 1 – 7: 42).

(3) Revolt of Judas; death of Antiochus; purification
of Temple (8: 1 – 10: 9).

(4) Continued fighting; defeat of Lysias; peace with
Antiochus V (10: 10 – 13: 26).

(5) Nicanor (14: 1 – 15: 36).[1]

The epitomist seems to have reproduced some of the
material in fairly full detail if it captured his attention and
held his interest; he may even have added moralizing
touches to it. Other material he considerably reduced
making only a catalogue-like summary. The story of the
martyrdom of the seven sons in chapter 7 may be mentioned as an example of fairly full reproduction, whereas
13: 19–26 offers an example of the way in which he summarized his source and recited the events in rapid succession. There is, however, very little evidence of real abridgment and one writer has been led to say: 'But, as II Maccabees has every appearance of being a rhetorical amplifi-
cation rather than a summary, it would not be surprising
if its alleged model existed only in the author's imagination'.[2]

The obvious didactic purpose of II Maccabees and the
almost certain disorder in the events narrated inevitably
detract from the objectivity of the book if it be regarded
simply as history. One cannot help but sense an element of
caricature about the stories of miraculous help from

[1] B. M. Metzger, *An Introduction to the Apocrypha*, 1957, p. 139, suggests the following verses as indicating the end of each of the five books:
3: 40, 7: 42, 10: 9, 13: 26 and 15: 27.

[2] Ch. Guignebert, *The Jewish World in the Time of Jesus*, 1939, p. 15.

heaven, and of the willingness of the martyrs to undergo extremes of torture for the sake of their religious beliefs with an utter disregard of the intensity of the suffering. But, like all caricatures, there is a very great deal of truth in them and we may well feel that the proper use of the book is as a pictorial supplement to I Maccabees.

The author is unknown, nor is it certain whether, after abridging the longer work, he was also responsible for adding the two letters at the beginning. It is fairly certain that he wrote in Greek. It is also commonly thought that the two letters may be translations of Hebrew originals. The letters are not integral parts of the book, they serve simply to provide a setting by urging the Egyptian community to celebrate the feast of Purification and reminding them of the miraculous way in which the altar fire was provided in the time of Nehemiah. A reference in the first letter to a letter written in 143 B.C. (the one hundred and sixty-ninth year of the Seleucid era) suggests that there was yet another letter not now extant.[1]

The place of writing can only be guessed at, there is no certain indication within the book. The fact that the author wrote in Greek points to Alexandria as a possible place of origin and this is supported by the inclusion of the letters to Egypt with which the book begins. Access to them would be natural in Egypt but not readily conceivable elsewhere.

We are no better informed about the date of writing. This undoubtedly turns on the date that might be established, speculatively, for Jason's history. But we know nothing at all about Jason beyond what is said in II Macc.

---

[1] A suggestion has been made that the letter referred to in 1: 7 is that recorded in 1: 10–2: 18 and that the date given in 1: 7 is a gloss. Bickermann, *Z.N.T.W.*, 1933, p. 233.

2: 23. He could be identified with the Jason who is mentioned in I Macc. 8: 17 as going on a mission to Rome, but this is pure conjecture. In the absence of any definite date it is left to the reader to infer the most likely date from the nature of the book and the lapse of time one might think it necessary to allow for a five-volume history to reach the stage of being epitomized. Some time in the first half of the first century B.C. would be a possible date.

Note on III and IV Maccabees

There are two other books of the Maccabees extant besides the two in the Apocrypha. III Maccabees is to be found in two Uncial MSS, A and V, and in some cursives, but it was not taken up into the Vulgate and did not therefore become part of the Apocrypha. It has, however, striking affinities with II Maccabees both in language, style and ideas, which, though not demanding identity of authorship, do suggest the same period of time and the same milieu. The book is entirely concerned with an attempt made by Ptolemy IV (Philopator) to enter Jerusalem at the time of the battle of Raphia in 217 B.C. He was repulsed and thereupon wreaked his vengeance on the Jews of Alexandria. IV Maccabees is cast in an entirely different mould, being a sort of lecture by an orthodox Jew, who was at the same time a student of Greek philosophy with leanings towards stoicism, on the theme that the four cardinal virtues can be attained through adherence to the Jewish Law. It offers the martyrdom of Eleazar as an example of true defiance of tyrants. This use of the Maccabean story as illustrative material is probably the only reason for its designation as IV Maccabees. It is to be found in three uncials, A, ℵ, V.

I

CHAPTER XV

THE OLD TESTAMENT IN THE APOCRYPHA

In the Old Testament itself there is recognition here and there, especially from the time of the Exile onwards, of the permanence and authority of some of the literature it contains. The law of Moses is appealed to as a written document in I Kings 2: 3 and elsewhere. The prophetic writings, particularly where prophecies remain unfulfilled, are recognized as having a validity which would extend at least until the time of fulfilment. The elders in the time of Jeremiah appealed to the oracles of Mica(ia)h more than a century earlier as a justification for their acquittal of Jeremiah. They made the appeal in a way that shows the oracles to have been remembered, if not written down, and to have been accepted as authoritative beyond temporal human authorship (Jer. 26: 17–19). The appeal to written prophecy is made quite explicit in Daniel: 'I, Daniel, perceived in the books the number of years which, according to the word of the Lord to Jeremiah the prophet, must pass before the end of the desolations of Jerusalem, namely, seventy years' (9: 2). Appeal to the word of the Lord by the mouth of Jeremiah is also made by the Chronicler (II Chron. 36: 21, 22; Ezra 1: 1). This indicates that by the time some of the latest books of the Old Testament were written both the law and the prophetic literature were held to be authoritative.

Among the apocryphal writers we find that there is a similar respect for the law and the prophets and also implicitly for other books like Psalms and Proverbs. They draw freely on the Old Testament for phrases, allusions and illustrations without feeling any need to acknowledge their source. There is an implicit recognition of the authority of the Old Testament writings.

Now and again, but very rarely, the authors openly acknowledge their recognition of the written word of God, as in Baruch 1: 20–21: '. . . the calamities and the curse which the Lord declared through Moses his servant at the time when he brought our fathers out of Egypt to give to us a land flowing with milk and honey. We did not heed the voice of the Lord our God in all the words of the prophets whom he sent to us . . .' and in Baruch 2: 28: '. . . as thou didst speak by thy servant Moses on the day when thou didst command him to write thy law in the presence of the people of Israel'. The author of Susanna is much more explicit when he makes Daniel say, in his accusation of one of the elders, 'condemning the innocent and letting the guilty go free, though the Lord said, "Do not put to death an innocent and righteous person"' (quoting Exod. 23: 7). Although for the most part the writers introduce their quotations and allusions without any distinguishing sign or word there is a place in Ecclesiasticus (9: 12) where ben Sira seems to draw attention to an allusion to Prov. 11: 21 with the imperative, 'Remember'.

I Esdras 1: 57, 58, 2: 1 repeat the Chronicler's reference to the words of the Lord by the mouth of Jeremiah (II Chron. 36: 21 f.) but in I Esdras 1: 28 the editor has an interesting misreading of the Chronicler's statement (II Chron. 35: 22) and instead of the phrase, 'He did not listen to the words of Neco from the mouth of God' he has, 'did not heed the words of Jeremiah the prophet from the mouth of the Lord'. The other explicit references to the Old Testament, a dozen all told, are to the book, or the law, of Moses, or simply to Moses (I Esdras 5: 49; 7: 6, 9; Tob. 7: 13; Bar. 2: 2; Sus: 3, 62; I Macc. 4: 47, 53; II Macc. 1: 29; 7: 6; 12: 40).

This is in striking contrast to the New Testament which speaks some fifty-three times of *scripture* or *the scriptures*, once saying that 'all scripture is inspired by God' (II Tim. 3: 16), which often links the law and the prophets, and which nearly four-score times refers to, or quotes the Old Testament, with a phrase such as 'as it is written'. One compelling reason for this difference is that the authors of the Apocrypha did not need to appeal to scripture in proof of what they were writing about. They were a group of writers for whom the Old Testament (although it is clearly an anachronism to speak of it thus as a unity in the time of the apocryphal writers) existed as a corpus of writings, all well-known and much of it very familiar, from which they drew their phrases and allusions. By their frequent use of its story, its thought and its words they show how firm a place the books of the Old Testament held in the intellectual and spiritual life of Israel in the pre-Christian centuries.

The following list of phrases contains but a selection of the many that are to be found scattered throughout the writings of the Apocrypha:

spare thy people	II Esdras 8:45	Joel 2: 17
turned its beauty into shame	Judith 1: 14	Hos. 4: 7
cover the face of the earth	Judith 2: 7; 7: 18	Num. 22:5, 11

looked upon their afflictions	Judith 4: 13	Exod. 3: 7
your God shall be my God	Judith 11: 23	Ruth 1: 16
wife of your bosom	Ecclus. 9: 1	Deut. 13: 6; 28: 54
valiant over wine	Ecclus. 31: 25.	Isa. 5: 22
flowing with milk and honey	Bar. 1: 20	Exod. 3: 8 &c.
robe of righteousness	Bar. 5: 2	Isa. 61: 10

The following list gives some of the more obvious allusions to Old Testament ideas and incidents:

vault of heaven	Ecclus. 24: 5	Job 22: 14
in rage he slew his brother	Wisd. 10: 3	Gen. 4: 8–13
the name that ought not to be shared	Wisd. 14: 21	Isa. 42: 8
cord of blue	Ecclus. 6: 30	Num. 15: 38
gold of Ophir	Ecclus. 7: 18	I Kgs. 9: 28
a signet with the Lord ...	Ecclus. 17: 22	Jer. 22: 24
the apple of his eye	Ecclus. 17: 22	Deut. 32: 10
abomination of desolation	I Macc. 1: 54	Dan. 11: 31
the blood that cried out	II Macc. 8: 3	Gen. 4: 10

Since much of the apocryphal material was written in Greek, it is not in the least surprising to find that the Greek translation of the Old Testament[1] was known and used. This may be seen in Judith 6: 2 where Isa. 28: 1, 2 in its Greek form seems to be the source for the phrase

[1] Commonly called the Septuagint, because of the legend that seventy-two Jewish scholars, six from each tribe, translated it.

'hirelings of Ephraim'; the Hebrew has 'drunkards of Ephraim'. The book of Wisdom shows the use of the Greek bible much more clearly; several places have already been mentioned where there is noticeable dependence (2: 12; 11: 4; 11: 22; 15: 10).[1]

This means that the apocryphal writers, who were keenly zealous for their religion, were steeped in the literature of that religion to such an extent that they fell readily into using its phrases and alluding to its contents without giving a second thought to what we might call 'canonical' implications. Sometimes two allusions occur within a single verse, as there seem to be in Wisd. 3: 7:

> In the time of their visitation they will shine forth,
> And will run like sparks through the stubble.

This refers to the righteous men exercising judgment on the wicked who are likened to stubble as in Obad. 18 through which the fire quickly runs as in Isa. 5: 24. A further double allusion may be seen in II Esdras 10: 22 which depends upon Isa. 24: 8 in its first two clauses and Lam. 5: 11, 13 in its final clause.

No literature will remain long without critics and we find a critical attitude to the Old Testament in at least three places. Psalm 8: 4 is parodied by the author of II Esdras in this way: 'But what is man, that thou art angry with him; or what is a corruptible race, that thou art so bitter against it' (8: 34). Ben Sira seems to have seized upon Lam. 3: 44, 'Thou hast wrapped thyself with a cloud so that no prayer can pass through' in order to deny its permanent validity, for in 35: 17 he wrote, 'The prayer of the humble pierces the clouds, and he will not be con-

[1] See p. 58.

soled until it reaches the Lord'. A third instance is Ecclus. 15: 9 where the idea of Psalm 33: 1 is reversed.

A further thing that may happen when the literature of previous generations or earlier centuries is freely drawn upon is that phrases may be used out of their context and gain fresh meaning or shade of meaning thereby. When ben Sira in 17: 3 alludes to Gen. 1: 26, 'and made them in his own image', he is using the phrase in its natural Hebraic sense as it is used in the first instance. But when the author of Wisdom uses it in 2: 23, 'and made him in the image of his own eternity', it is in a Greek setting and has reference to the fact that immortality, in Greek thought, is the essence of Godhead. This is likely to be all the more true when the writer is writing Greek and using translations of Hebrew words and phrases. It happens quite often in the book of Wisdom where the Old Testament conceptions of man, of the body, soul and spirit are taken up by the writer into his Greek arguments. But it is not only with Hebrew phrases that this happens. A Platonic phrase is used in the book of Wisdom (11: 17) 'out of formless matter', but the author is not thereby subscribing to the Platonic doctrine of the creation of the world out of formless matter, he is simply enhancing the power of God by implying that God can contain in himself all the power that philosophers might think it takes to make the world.

A rough and ready calculation of the number of references or allusions to each of the books of the Old Testament in the Apocrypha yields the following result. The most loved and widely used book was the book of Psalms. Next comes Proverbs, but this is offset by the fact that nearly all allusions or possible allusions to the book are in Ecclesiasticus (136 out of 166), so that in reality it was not necessarily the second in popularity. Exodus would also

have a claim to high popularity were it not that the book
of Wisdom accounts for half the instances, mainly because
its subject matter makes many allusions to the Egyptian
period of Israelite history inevitable. Isaiah was a well-
used book, a fact which is attested also by the discovery
of the Dead Sea Scrolls among which 'Isaiah is easily the
most frequently found' of prophetic books.[1] One of the
lesser used books is that of Judges; even ben Sira, who
might have been expected to use it for several members of
his roll of famous men, has only two verses about the
judges:

> The judges also, with their respective names,
> Those whose hearts did not fall into idolatry
> And who did not turn away from the Lord—
> May their memory be blessed!
> May their bones revive from where they lie,
> And may the name of those who have been honoured
> Live again in their sons! (46: 11, 12)

Although they knew the books of the Old Testament
very well indeed and drew from them at large, there is not
much evidence to show that the apocryphal writers
thought of them as a more or less closed and completed
body of sacred literature.[2] The law had come down to
them in a fixed form; but that had been so since the days
of the Exile. They knew that the line of prophets had come
to an end and that there could be no more prophetic literature. Three times in I Maccabees the absence of a prophet

---

[1] J. T. Milik, *Ten Years of Discovery in the Wilderness of Judaea*, 1959,
p. 26.

[2] The Prologue to Ecclesiasticus comes nearest to such recognition in
the well-known phrase, 'the law, the prophets and the other books of our
fathers'; and in the book itself there is reference to 'the law of the Most
High. . . . The wisdom of all the ancients, and . . . prophecies' (39: 1).

was bemoaned: in 4: 46 where the stones of the defiled altar were to be stored 'in a convenient place on the temple hill until there should come a prophet to tell what to do with them'; in 9: 27 great distress is reported 'such as had not been since the time that prophets ceased to appear among them'; and 14: 41 which refers to Simon as 'their leader and high priest for ever, until a trustworthy prophet should arise'. Even ben Sira, who shows more awareness of the limits of the Old Testament than any other writer, is not interested in the books but in the men in them. It was the succession of inspired leaders, the prophets in particular, which mattered to him. But whether the writers knew it or not there is no doubt that they stood at one of the turning points in the making of Scripture. They came at the end of the chapter, indeed, at the end of an age. In many ways they help us to pass easily from the age of expectation represented by the Old Testament to the age of fulfilment represented by the New Testament.

CHAPTER XVI

THE APOCRYPHA IN THE CHURCH

(i) THE USE OF THE TERM APOCRYPHA

THE word Apocrypha is in form the neuter plural of the Greek word *apocryphos* meaning 'hidden'. It has been used in two different ways when applied to literature. First, it has been used to designate writings which ought not to be circulated outside a limited circle because of the mysterious or esoteric or magical nature of their contents. In this sense the book of Revelation has been designated as 'apocryphal'.[1] Second, it has been used to designate any book or writing which was withheld from publication or circulation for any reason whatever, usually because of some uncertainty about its authorship, or something questionable about its teaching. In this usage it came to have the connotation 'spurious'. It can therefore either imply books *not included* or books *deliberately excluded* according to the approach one makes to it.

The use of the word Apocrypha as a technical term for those books which now form an appendix to the Old Testament appears to have been used first by Jerome in his *Prologus Galeatus*,[2] but it did not come into regular use until the sixteenth century when Andreas Bodenstein[3]

---

[1] By Gregory of Nyssa.

[2] I.e. the preface to his translation of Samuel and Kings.

[3] Commonly called Karlstadt after the name of his birthplace. He wrote a discussion of the canon in *De Canonicis Scripturis Libellus* (1520).

(born in 1480) re-introduced it. Since then the word has been in general use among Protestants to designate the books on the margin of the canon and coming between the Old and New Testaments.

Catholics, on the other hand, use the term 'deutero-canonical' to describe these books and reserve the term Apocrypha for the later books which were never a part of the canon and are often called Pseudepigrapha (i.e. books falsely entitled).

(ii) THE JEWS AND THE APOCRYPHAL BOOKS

The Jews do not seem to have accorded the books of the Apocrypha any greater status than that of any other 'profane' literature. This statement however must be qualified by the reminder that it was only at a comparatively late date that the idea of a 'closed' canon of scripture emerged. We have seen that much of the material in the Apocrypha was being written at a time when the third part of the canon of the Old Testament was still unsettled and incomplete. Any book written during the first half of that time or even later might have stood a chance of finding its way into the canon. When ben Sira's grandson translated Ecclesiasticus into Greek (c. 132 B.C.) he spoke of the scriptures as 'the law and the prophets and the other books of our fathers'. Philo has a similar phrase in *De Vita Contemplativa*, 'laws and oracles delivered through the mouth of prophets, and psalms and anything else (or, the other books) which fosters and perfects knowledge and piety' (Loeb edition, vol. IX, p. 127). With that we may compare Luke 24: 44, 'the law of Moses and the prophets and the psalms'. Towards the end of the first century A.D. we find a more definite statement in Josephus: 'we do not possess myriads of inconsistent books, conflicting with each other. Our

books, those which are justly accredited, are but two and
twenty, and contain the record of all time. Of these, five
are the books of Moses . . . the prophets subsequent to
Moses wrote the history of the events of their own times in
thirteen books. The remaining four[1] books contain hymns
to God and precepts for the conduct of human life' (*Contra
Apionem*. Loeb ed., vol. I, p. 179). This gives a total of
twenty-two, corresponding with the number of letters in
the Hebrew alphabet. II Esdras 14: 44–47 counts them as
twenty-four: 'Make public the twenty-four books that you
wrote first and let the worthy and the unworthy read them;
but keep the seventy that were written last, in order to
give them to the wise among your people.' Whether we
count them as twenty-two (linking Ruth with Judges and
Lamentations with Jeremiah) or as twenty-four, it is clear
that this represents the Old Testament as we know it.
This is frequently spoken of as the Palestinian or Hebrew
Canon.

The evidence of the discoveries at Qumrân suggests that
in that community at least there was no serious attempt at
segregating the canonical books from the others. Fragments of two if not three of the apocryphal books have
been found: Tobit, Ecclesiasticus and possibly The Letter
of Jeremiah (in Greek). But there are books and fragments
of other literature as well, some known elsewhere (Jubilees,
Enoch, the Testament of the Twelve Patriarchs) and some
peculiar to the community (Manual of Discipline, War of
the Sons of Light with the Sons of Darkness, and certain
commentaries). The community centre was destroyed by
enemy attack in A.D. 68 and this was followed by fire. The
scrolls may have been put in the caves for safety at that

---

[1] These four are probably Psalms, Song of Songs, Proverbs and
Ecclesiastes.

time, or the caves may have been their permanent store place; at all events the literary stock of the community in the middle of the first century is indicated by the discoveries.

At the end of the first century Jewish scholars meeting together at Jamnia in council or in academic session discussed the inclusion or exclusion of a number of books from the corpus of sacred literature. They did not pronounce on the canonical books as a whole; they tacitly accepted those about which no doubt existed, and discussed those which had been disputed, among them Ezekiel, Ecclesiastes, the Song of Songs and Esther. It is quite clear that by the end of the first century the Jews had reached a common mind on the books to be regarded as the sacred writings with only slight marginal differences of opinion. It has to be remembered that up to this time, and for some time yet to come, the books of the Old Testament in their Hebrew form were not written together within a single volume or scroll. They were written separately on scrolls, e.g. the five separate books of the Torah, or in groups, e.g. the prophecies collected under the name of Isaiah, or the book of the twelve (minor) prophets. Outwardly there was probably nothing to distinguish them from any of the other writings which did not enter into the collection of sacred writings. Some of the books of the Apocrypha were written in Hebrew and took their place among this miscellaneous collection of writings but do not seem ever to have come into the special category of 'sacred'.

When these books found their way to the Jews of the Dispersion they would be translated into Greek in the same way as the canonical books were. Ben Sira's grandson has left us record of such translation in the prologue to his grandfather's book which he himself translated. A further record of translation, probably that of the canonical book of Esther, is found in the Additions to Esther (11: 1). Other books of the Apocrypha were written in Greek in Alexandria, but there is no reason to suppose that these, any more than those in Hebrew, were ever included among the sacred books by the Jews. What is reasonable to suppose is that men would have their favourites among the non-canonical books just as they did among the canonical books.

(iii) THE APOCRYPHA IN THE CHRISTIAN CHURCH TO 1520

The Christian Church inherited the writings of the Jews as they inherited from them so much else, but they inevitably had a different regard for them since they read them in the light of the Gospel.

At the same time, however, a new factor emerged which probably had a great deal to do with the formation of the canon of scripture. This new factor was that the Christians began to write their literature in book form—codices—as distinct from rolls. As far as may be judged from the evidence they may have begun to use codices as early as the first century. The immediate advantage of the codex over the roll was that more could be written down within a single compass than had ever been possible with rolls where great length was impracticable. It seems therefore that it was in the Christian church that the books of the Old Testament were first collected into book form. The evidence of the three great codices, Vaticanus and Sinaiticus in the fourth century and Alexandrinus in the fifth, shows that there was no fixed order of the books, except that the Law came first, that the Christians were already collecting and incorporating some extra-canonical (apocryphal) books, that they were not rigid about the order in which they placed them, that they did not relegate them to an appendix to the Old Testament, and lastly that there was no fixed tradition as to which extra-canonical books to include. The following lists of the contents of these three codices will illustrate the diversity of usage.

Codex Vaticanus: Gen.-Deut., Josh., Judg., Ruth, I–IV Kingd., Chron., Ezra-Neh., Psalms, Prov., Eccles., Song of Songs, Job, Wisdom, Ecclus., Esther, Judith, Tobit, Hosea, Amos, Mic., Joel, Obad., Jon., Nah., Hab., Zeph., Hag., Zech., Mal., Isa., Jer., Baruch, Lam., Letter of Jeremiah, Ezek., Daniel.

Codex Sinaiticus: Fragments of Gen. and Num., I Chron. 9: 27 – 19: 17, II Esdras (Ezr.-Neh.) 9: 9–end, Esther, Tobit, Judith, I Maccabees, IV Maccabees, Isa., Jer., Lam., Joel, Obad., Jon., Nah., Hab., Zeph., Hag., Zech., Mal., Psalms, Prov., Eccles., Song of Songs, Wisdom, Ecclus., Job.

Codex Alexandrinus: Gen.-Deut., Josh., Judg., Ruth, I–IV Kingd., Chron., 12 minor prophets, Isa., Jer., Baruch, Lam., Letter of Jeremiah, Ezek., Dan., Esther, Tobit, Judith, I and II Esdras, I–IV Maccabees, Psalms, Odes,[1] Job, Prov., Eccles., Song of Songs, Wisdom, Ecclus., Psalms of Solomon (listed only at end of table of contents).

The fact that these codices, or rather their earlier predecessors, included many books, or parts of books, that had not hitherto received special recognition would probably be an incentive to Jewish scholars to define more closely the limits of their canonical books. It also meant, however, that new books were being put forward with a virtual claim for recognition.

---

[1] A collection of certain poetic passages such as the Song of Miriam, the Psalm of Jonah, the Magnificat and (from the Apocrypha) the Prayer of Manasseh.

If these codices are Christian products it is not right to infer from them that the Jews of the Dispersion held to a different canon of scripture from their Palestinian brethren. Nevertheless the collection that includes the apocryphal books is frequently spoken of as the Alexandrian canon as distinct from the Palestinian (or Hebrew) canon. The apocryphal books, however, were not uniformly recognized by Christians in the early centuries. Melito, Bishop of Sardis (c. A.D. 170) set down a list of the Old Testament scriptures which agrees with the Hebrew canon, except that it does not include Esther. Origen's list also follows the Hebrew canon and also omits Esther, but it includes with Jeremiah a work called 'the Epistle', and this may be either the Letter of Jeremiah or the book of Baruch. Athanasius (d. 373) gives a list in which Jeremiah is followed by Baruch, Lamentations and the Letter of Jeremiah, and adds a note to the effect that some outside the canon are to be recommended for reading: Wisdom, Ecclus., Esther, Judith, Tobit. This implies that although the extra-canonical books were being written down in the same volumes as the canonical ones, many Christian leaders distinguished between them.

When Jerome (346–426) made his translation, which became the official Latin Bible, the Vulgate, he became dissatisfied with making a translation of a translation (the Septuagint) and, having learned Hebrew in his earlier years, decided to translate from the Hebrew text. This introduced him to the narrower limits of the Hebrew canon with which he found himself in full sympathy, so that he tended to skimp his work on the extra-canonical books. In prefaces which he wrote to the books he drew attention to the difference between the books that were canonical and those that were edifying. However, his view did not prevail

officially, and the Latin Bible came to include all the books
now found in the Apocrypha.[1]

The implication of this is that, practically speaking, the
Christian Church in the early centuries accepted the witness of the Greek Bible and included the apocryphal books
in the canon of the Old Testament. This remained so until
the sixteenth century. There were, it is true, some dissen-
tient voices. As has been mentioned, Jerome himself would
have followed the Hebrew practice if the tradition of the
church had not been too strong for him. Origen (186–253)
and Africanus (first half of third century) also recognized
some difference between the books in the Hebrew canon
and the additional books in the Greek Bible. But most of
the church fathers, familiar with the Greek Bible, followed
that tradition and accepted the longer canon without
demur. Augustine (354–430), for example, frequently
quotes apocryphal books as if they held the same authority
as other books of the Old Testament. Between these two
extremes there is a compromise, first clearly stated by
Rufinus (d. 410), which regards the apocryphal books as
'ecclesiastical' and useful for moral purposes, or, as Article
VI in the Anglican Prayer Book expresses it, 'the other
books the church doth read for example of life and instruction of manners'.

(iv) 1520 TO THE PRESENT DAY

In the sixteenth century there came a change of outlook
and emphasis regarding the scriptures. More attention was
paid to them as the fundamental basis of church life and
doctrine, and their limits were subjected to closer scrutiny
than had been given them for many a century. The change

---

[1] See H. F. D. Sparks' essay on the Latin Bible in *The Bible in its
English and Ancient Versions*, ed. by H. W. Robinson, 1940.

K

began with the teaching and influence of two men, both
eager students of scripture. Karlstadt (b. 1480) and Luther
(1483–1546) had been fellow students at Erfurt and became colleagues at Wittenberg. Karlstadt took part in the
discussion that ensued when Luther nailed his theses to
the church door at Wittenberg in 1517. He declared that
the Bible was the ultimate rule of faith. This meant that
there must be a proper examination and definition of the
documents involved and of the nature of canonicity. This
he did in a book published in 1520 called *De Canonicis
Scripturis Libellus*. His position was that the Old Testament canon should be restricted to the books of the
Hebrew canon, as Jerome had clearly shown. The books of
the Apocrypha Karlstadt divided into two groups: (i) Wisdom, Ecclus., Judith, Tobit, I and II Maccabees; these,
though apocryphal, are also hagiographa (sacred writings)
and thus have some value; and (ii) I and II Esdras, Baruch,
the Prayer of Manasseh, a large part of Daniel 3 and the last
two chapters of Daniel;[1] these are plainly apocryphal. He
used the word apocryphal with reference to the hidden and
unknown origin of the books and therefore as not included
in the canon. Luther's own view more or less coincided
with this, but was less academic and much more subjective.
In effect he separated the books of the Apocrypha as being
merely books that were allowed to be read, and introduced
them with the words, 'These are books not to be held in
equal esteem with those of Holy Scripture but yet good and
useful for reading'. He also suggested that Esther, Ecclesiastes and Chronicles ought to have been excluded from the
canon and that I Maccabees should have been included.[2]

---

[1] I.e. Susanna and Bel and the Dragon.

[2] This view, though purely subjective is one that commands assent
and compels comparison of these books with others in the Apocrypha

It is a curious fact that the church, East or West, Catholic or Protestant, has been very reluctant to make formal pronouncement on the books of the Apocrypha, but in view of this reluctance it is not surprising to find, as we do, that there was no uniformity in the manner in which the apocryphal books were treated and how and where they were placed in the Bible. There finally came a day when the Old Testament and the New Testament were printed together without the Apocrypha. The first official statement came from the Council of Trent in 1546, which decreed the exclusive use of the Vulgate, which contained the books of the Bible as accepted by the church, i.e. as found in the Greek Bible. For some reason three books, though found in many MSS of the Vulgate, were denied canonical status: the Prayer of Manesseh and I and II Esdras. The other apocryphal books continued to occupy the place they had for long held, scattered among the other books. It was extensively revised by a papal commission. The revision was printed in 1592 under Clement VIII. It shows that there was some reluctance in accepting the decision of the Council of Trent in its entirety for it contained the Prayer of Manasseh and I and II Esdras printed after the New Testament (and thus avoiding their total loss, while making a show at keeping to the decision of the Council).

The Greek church, on the other hand, seems to have had difficulty in coming to a common mind, but at a Synod in Jerusalem in 1672 four apocryphal books were accepted into the canon: Wisdom, Ecclus., Tobit, Judith.[1]

As early as 1522, however, Bibles were printed in which

---

which might well claim precedence for their usefulness in worship and in private devotion.

[1] I.e. four of the books which Karlstadt put in his first group.

the apocryphal books were distinguished from the rest. In that year, that is, two years after Karlstadt's book was published, a Lutheran evangelist named Andreas Osiander prepared and published a copy of the Vulgate in which he adopted Karlstadt's views by indicating which books were not in the Hebrew canon. In the edition of the Aldine Greek Bible printed at Strasbourg in 1524–26 Luther's example was followed and the apocryphal books were separated and inserted between the Old Testament and the New Testament. The reformers in Switzerland produced the Zürich Bible between 1527 and 1529; this was in six volumes of which the fifth contained the Apocrypha, prefaced by the words 'These are the books which are not reckoned as Biblical by the ancients, nor are found among the Hebrews'. In 1534 Luther's translation appeared with the apocryphal books printed after the Old Testament. I and II Esdras were omitted by him because 'they contained absolutely nothing which one could not much more easily find in Aesop or even in more trivial books'.[1] The section of apocryphal books is headed: 'Apocrypha, that is, books which are not held equal to the Holy Scriptures, and yet are profitable and good to read'.

The story of the printing of the Bible and Apocrypha in English is a strange and fascinating one and illustrates, among other things, the English genius for letting things take their own course. In his English translation Coverdale followed the continental reformers in separating the Apocrypha and in calling it by that name. On the second title page he explains his attitude to the books of the Apocrypha which have 'many places in them that seem repugnant unto the open and manifest truth in the other books of the

---

[1] Preface to Baruch. Later editions of the Luther Bible, however, did contain these books.

Bible . . . let the Holy Ghost be thy teacher, and let one
text expound another unto thee'. In 1534 while Coverdale
was preparing his translation, Convocation made a peti-
tion to the king that 'the holy scripture shall be translated
into the vulgar English tongue by certain upright and
learned men to be named by the said most illustrious King
and be meted out and delivered to the people for their instruction'. Coverdale's Bible was not what Convocation
expressly asked for, but it served the purpose, although it
received no official authorization, and was published in
1535. Convocation cannot have been fully satisfied with it,
for in 1536 they petitioned the king for a new translation.
A new edition of Coverdale in 1537 has on its title page,
'Set forth with the king's most gracious licence'. The significant thing about this is that though the royal licence
would greatly assist the sale of the Bible, it did not give it
ecclesiastical sanction; neither Convocation nor other
church leaders were consulted—Henry acted either on his
own initiative, or, more probably, under prompting from
Thomas Cromwell.

In the same year, 1537, John Rogers published another
English Bible, known as Matthew's Bible. It was printed
abroad, followed Coverdale in the matter of the order of
the books and the separation of the Apocrypha from the
rest, and incorporated parts of Coverdale's translation and
parts of Tyndale's. Cranmer wrote to Cromwell urging him
to show this Bible to the king and get him to license it.
The title page therefore has the words: 'Set forth with the
king's most gracious licence'. It differed from Coverdale's
Bible in removing Baruch from its position after Jeremiah
to the Apocrypha, where it follows Ecclus. and in including
the Prayer of Manasseh (taken, in all probability, from the
French Bible edited by Olivetan, 1535). Matthew's Bible

also reproduced from Olivetan's Bible a note on the separation of the Apocrypha which, in an English translation, was printed behind the second title page (i.e. following Malachi).

These Bibles mark a turning point. For the first time in England Bibles were issued which gathered the books of the Apocrypha together. Matthew's Bible did this more completely than Coverdale's since it put Baruch also in the Apocrypha. No authority had been given for this at any time; it happened as the result of successive editings and the exercise of personal judgment. The Apocrypha was now once and for all relegated to a secondary place and the time was not far distant when it would cease to be printed as part of the Bible. The royal ordinance of 1538 ordering every curate to see that a Bible 'of the largest volume in English' was set up in every church meant that Matthew's Bible (two inches longer than Coverdale's) with its complete separation of the Apocrypha became the normal church Bible.

Eventually, in 1599, and probably by simple accident, an edition of the Geneva Bible[1] was published without the Apocrypha. Apparently it happened during the binding processes, for the titles of the books of the Apocrypha appear at the beginning of the Bible and are crossed out in ink. This must have set up a precedent which binders were not slow to take advantage of, for, although it was not till 1640 that a version of the Geneva Bible appeared in which the Apocrypha was deliberately omitted,[2] Archbishop Abbot thought it necessary in 1615 to forbid any stationer from issuing a Bible without the Apocrypha under penalty

[1] Translated at Geneva by a group of reformers who had fled from threatened persecution under Queen Mary, and first published in 1560.

[2] A statement about its omission was inserted between Malachi and the New Testament.

of a year's imprisonment.[1] The authorized version of 1611 followed the prevailing practice and printed the Apocrypha under that title as a separate part of the Bible between the Old and New Testaments. Copies of King James' Bible did appear, however, without the Apocrypha in 1626, 1629, 1630 and 1633.

The situation was reflected in the Book of Common Prayer and in public discussion. It was natural and proper that while the Apocrypha was regarded as an integral part of the Bible the service orders and the lectionary should regularly use it. Cartwright[2] and Whitgift[3] were in controversy over this very fact. Cartwright complained that some parts of the canonical books were omitted while place was given to apocryphal passages. Whitgift argued that this was as it should be because the Apocrypha had for all time been reckoned by the church among the canonical books. This was in 1572. In 1589 John Penry (under the name of Martin Marprelate) also joined in the discussion and argued in one of his tracts that the Bible should contain only those books which were held to be absolutely inspired. But, as we have seen, the situation was slowly changing, and in 1644 'Parliament issued regulations about public worship and ordered that all the canonical books of the Old and New Testaments (but none of those which are commonly called Apocrypha) were to be publicly read in the vulgar tongue'.[4]

---

[1] Edward Arber, *A Transcript of the Register of the Company of Stationers of London*, vol. V (Birmingham, 1894), p. xlix. (Ref. in Howorth's article 'The Anglican Canon, its Origin and Authority', *J.T.S.*, vol. VIII, p. 35.)

[2] Professor of Divinity at Cambridge in 1572.

[3] Archbishop of Canterbury, 1583–1604.

[4] See Sir H. H. Howorth: 'The Origin and Authority of the Biblical Canon in the Anglican Church', *J.T.S.*, VIII, pp. 1–40, upon which this section has largely drawn.

Thus the Apocrypha was at last set aside. The Westminster Confession (1648), representative of nonconformist belief, states this with simple clarity: 'The books commonly called Apocrypha not being of divine inspiration are no part of the canon of the scripture, and therefore are of no authority in the church of God, nor to be in any wise approved or made use of, than other human writings'. In 1666 Field published a Bible at Cambridge entitled 'The Old and New Testament without the Apocrypha'.

In the Church of England a compromise had been reached. The Apocrypha had been relegated to a secondary place contrary to the usage of the early church and without any official ecclesiastical sanction. Article VI in the prayer book speaks of 'those canonical books of the Old and New Testament, of whose Authority was never any doubt in the church' . . . then of the Apocrypha it goes on to say, 'and the other books (as Hierome saith) the church doth read for example of life and instruction of manners; but yet doth it not apply them to establish any doctrine'. On the other hand in Article XXXV two books of homilies are commended because of their good and wholesome doctrine, although some of these homilies contain references to the books of the Apocrypha and quote passages from them as if they were on the same footing as the canonical books, which is exactly what the church had been accustomed to.

There are two well-known literary records of the use of the Apocrypha in the seventeenth century. The first is that of John Bunyan recording an experience of his in 1652. 'For thus it was expounded to me: Begin at the beginning of Genesis, and read to the end of the Revelations, and see if you can find, that there were ever any that trusted in the Lord, and were confounded. So coming home, I presently went to my Bible, to see if I could find that saying, not doubting but to find it presently. . . . Well, I looked but I found it not. . . . Thus I continued above a year, and could not find the place; but at last, casting my eye upon the Apocrypha books, I found it in Ecclesiasticus ii. 10. This, at the first, did somewhat daunt me; but because by this time I had got more experience of the love and kindness of God, it troubled me the less, especially when I considered that though it was not in those texts that we call holy and canonical; yet forasmuch as this sentence was the sum and substance of many of the promises, it was my duty to take the comfort of it; and I bless God for that word, for it was of God to me: that word doth still at times shine before my face.'[1]

Seven years later, in his diary for 1659–60, Samuel Pepys recorded (Feb. 5th) 'Church in the afternoon . . . a stranger preached a poor sermon, and so I read over the whole book of the story of Tobit'.[2]

The final stage in the rejection of the Apocrypha may be deemed to have come in 1827. In that year the Bible Society, under pressure from evangelicals, nonconformists and Scotch Presbyterians, decided not to print the Apocrypha nor to subscribe funds to any society that did print it. This affected several continental societies which still printed the Apocrypha. It also led to some embarrassment shortly before the coronation of King Edward VII, for it was discovered that the special Bible prepared by the British and Foreign Bible Society did not contain the Apocrypha and another copy had to be secured. Archbishop Temple pronounced the Bible without Apocrypha to be mutilated and imperfect.

[1] *Grace Abounding*, Paragraphs 63–65.
[2] Quoted by B. M. Metzger, *An Introduction to the Apocrypha*, 1957, pp. 198 f.

It is no wonder that, with such a history of doubt and uncertainty, the Apocrypha should tend to be neglected. Complaints have been levelled, and not without reason, at the standard of translation in both the Authorized and the Revised Versions. It has always been easy to make a Cinderella of the Apocrypha. The Revised Standard Version, fortunately, has not been guilty of so much neglect.[1]

[1] The new English Translation now in preparation is also giving proper attention to the books of the Apocrypha.

CHAPTER XVII

THE MERIT AND WORTH OF THE APOCRYPHA

THE books of the Apocrypha would command our attention even if the most we could say of them is that they are relics of the literature of the Jewish people, both in Palestine and in the Dispersion, of the period 300 B.C. to A.D. 100. But that is not all that can be said of them. Although there was other literature produced during those centuries, for one reason or another these books came to be regarded as being in a different category from some of the other books of the same period. They have been singled out by former generations of worshippers and scholars in the Christian Church as being 'useful and good to read' and as having value 'for example of life and instruction of manners'. One branch of the church has consistently revered them and ranked them as next to the Old Testament in scriptural authority.

They command our attention chiefly for a reason that may be said to spring out of both of these facts: they are the product of the generations after the close of the Old Testament writings and they supplement those writings in various ways; they are also the product of the last few generations before the Christian revelation and the writing of the New Testament books, and they therefore complement the Old Testament writings in their capacity of preparation for Christ. Herein lies their intrinsic merit, that

they are complementary documents to the Old Testament
and at the same time help to build up a clearer anticipation
of the Incarnation.

In what ways are they complementary? Briefly speaking, in the effects brought about by a transition from the
Hebrew to the Greek thought worlds and in the development of ideas which are scarcely, if at all, present in the
Old Testament but are at the very centre of New Testament thought. The documents of the Apocrypha are all
Jewish documents, with the exception of the four chapters
in II Esdras that are Christian additions. Some were written in Hebrew, some in Greek. They stand between the
Old Testament, which was written in Hebrew, except for
certain chapters of Aramaic in Ezra and Daniel,[1] and the
New Testament which was written in Greek.[2] They belong
essentially to an age of transition with one foot firmly
placed in Hebrew country, and the other seeking to gain
an equally firm footing in the Greek world, wherein the
future lay. The Hebrew documents in the Apocrypha were,
for the most part, written in Palestine, but the Greek
documents were probably written by Greek-speaking
Jews of the Dispersion and in all likelihood in Alexandria.
In the Dispersion the Jews were under the necessity of
presenting their thought in a Greek dress. These Greek
writers were continuing what had been begun in the
Greek translation of the Old Testament. One feature of the
process is that the full connotation of Hebrew words was
not always carried by the synonyms used to translate them
in Greek and at the same time the Greek words might well
carry more meaning, or a different nuance of meaning

[1] Dan. 2: 4 – 7: 28; Ezra 4: 8 – 6: 18, 7: 12–26; Jer. 10: 11 and two
words in Gen. 31: 47.

[2] This does not overlook the very strong probability that many of the
sayings of Jesus in the Gospels may have come from an Aramaic source.

from that borne by the original Hebrew. Thus a certain tension between Hebrew and Greek thought was inevitable. An example may be seen very clearly in the Book of Wisdom, notably in 8: 19, where the author begins with a statement that would be acceptable to any Hebrew thinker, even to one like ben Sira who shows himself completely untouched by Greek culture. The verse runs: 'As a child I was by nature well endowed, and a good soul fell to my lot'. Here we may detect the characteristic idea of the self-hood of the whole man, body animated by God-given soul which gave it spiritual vigour. But the next verse goes on 'or rather, being good, I entered an undefiled body'. This reflects the way a Greek might think of man, a body of flesh, corruptible, and merely the temporary home of the soul, pre-existent and incorruptible. We have already seen in discussing the book of Wisdom that we cannot always be quite sure whether to take what the author says in Greek at its full value or not, and this is mainly because he is still thinking in Hebrew ways but is using Greek words to express his thought. When St. Paul does much the same kind of thing and writes in Greek, though he is a 'Hebrew of the Hebrews', there is far less tension observable.

One of the ways in which the Apocrypha helps to fill in the thought area between the Old and New Testaments is in the field of mediation between God and man. Whether it came about under the influence of Greek thought or not, there was an increasing appreciation of God's aloofness from the world of men in the age that is represented by the apocryphal literature. One of the main features of apocalyptic writings which may be said to have originated in the same period (and are represented in the Apocrypha by II Esdras) is that of a catastrophic intervention in the affairs of men by God who dwells apart from it. Doubtless one of the reasons for the pseudonymity of apocalyptic writers is just this, that they are writing of things that in effect belong to God's world, that other world so far removed from this, and only those who have been there, or rather are there, like the righteous men of old, especially those whose removal from earth was by being taken up into the heavens, can tell of the things that belong to it. This recognition of God's aloofness led in turn to a growing need for mediatory elements between God and man. One of the urgent demands of religious life is that God should be in some way immediately accessible to men. If he is too far removed for this, then there must be some way of representing him among men. This need was met in two ways in the apocryphal writings. First in the belief in an angelic host and second in the idea of the personified and possibly hypostasized Wisdom of God.

The idea of an angelic host was not alien to the Old Testament, but, apart from the book of Daniel, it appears there in a very simple form without elaboration. There was one figure, the Angel of the Lord, who frequently took the place of God on occasions of intimate connection between God and men. He is always so called and is never identified by a proper name; indeed, in every place where he is mentioned it is clear that he is every bit in place of God and that in effect the distinction between him and God is purely a literary one. There is also a heavenly host whose members form God's court and are his messengers to carry out his orders. In the book of Daniel there is a very much more developed picture which is comparable with that in the book of Tobit. Daniel, being one of the latest of the Old Testament books, and being also an apocalypse, is much more a part of the apocryphal background than of that of the rest of the Old Testament. In Daniel God is said to be

surrounded by ten thousand times ten thousand who stood
before him (7: 10) and to send his angel to guard men
(3: 25, 28; 6: 22). The watchers and holy ones are mediators
between heaven and earth (4: 13, 17, 23, 31) and two angels
are mentioned by name, Gabriel (8: 15 f.) and Michael
(10: 13). The story of Tobit has the angel Raphael as one
of its central figures. He is described as 'one of the seven
holy angels, who present the prayers of the saints and enter into the presence of the glory of the Holy One' (12: 15).
There is also a strong background of belief in guardian
angels in the book. Raguel in joy invokes the 'angels and
chosen people' to bless God (8: 15) and Tobit says 'Blessed
are all thy holy angels' (11: 14). In ignorance at Raphael's
identity, Tobit dismisses Tobias on his journey with the
words 'God . . . prosper your journey and may his angel
go with thee' (5: 16) and to his wife he said 'Do not worry
. . . for a good angel will go with him; his journey will be
successful, and he will come back safe and sound' (5: 21).
It is not to be wondered at that a book with so clear a belief
in guardian angels should also have an equally vivid belief
in an evil demon in the figure of Asmodeus who caused the
death of Sarah's seven husbands (3: 8) but who could be
exorcized with the smoke of the heart and liver of the fish
(6: 7) and could be bound by Raphael (8: 3). One of the
underlying themes of II Maccabees is that of God sending
'manifestations' from heaven at such times as his people
were hard-pressed and had cried to him in their trouble.
The author says 'they besought the Lord to send a good
angel to save Israel' (11: 6; cf. 15: 23 'send a good angel to
carry terror and trembling before us').

The second way of mediation was that of the personified
figure of wisdom. A full description of this conception has
been given in the chapter on the book of Wisdom. In

brief, wisdom was conceived as a go-between, being present and assisting God at creation, conveying the knowledge of him to those who were fortunate enough to possess her and enabling them to become 'friends of God' (7: 27). In the triple role, as mediator of creation, inspiration and salvation, the figure of wisdom is able to take up into itself some of the earlier Old Testament ideas of mediation such as those of word, angel and spirit. It is a much discussed question whether the conception as found in the books of Wisdom and Ecclesiasticus may be properly described as a hypostasis, that is, a being conceived as having an independent existence apart from God, or a mere personification of one of God's attributes. The language of the book of Wisdom certainly gives a strong impression of hypostasization:

Wisdom is more mobile than any motion;
Because of her pureness she pervades and penetrates all things . . .
While remaining in herself, she renews all things;
In every generation she passes into holy souls,
And makes them friends of God, and prophets. (7: 24, 27)

A further fact which may be said to point towards hypostasization is the identity of Wisdom with the book of the law. This identification is made explicitly in Ecclus. 24: 23 and in Bar. 4: 1. No one could fail to appreciate the fact that the law was a written deposit of God's recorded will. Originally pronounced by him it was now embodied in a book and treasured among men. The identification of Wisdom with the law must surely imply that wisdom too could be regarded as having been sent by God to men to have a permanent home among them, or at least among such of them as revered God ('The fear of God is the beginning of wisdom'). Perhaps more significant than its possible bearing on the question of personification or hypostasization is the implication that, since the law was the only valid revelation of God and of his will, wisdom was of unique importance as its handmaid and interpreter.

This comes closer to the Christian revelation of Christ as mediator than any other Hebrew conception, for it is the most comprehensive and universal of any idea so far conceived. What is more, being personal, one may suppose that it had infinite possibilities. It comprised creative, revelatory and redemptive functions, that is to say, apparently all that was necessary for salvation. There is, however, one supreme difference between this conception of mediation and that of the Christian revelation: both the Hebrew and the Greek words for wisdom are feminine and the conception was, of necessity, a feminine figure. Wisdom could be identified with the law but could never have been identified with God. Nevertheless, there can be little doubt that such a conception of a mediatory figure was a true preparation for a Gospel of the Incarnation, in that men were not unprepared for the coming to earth of a heavenly power in personal form.

The doctrine of resurrection holds a central place in the Christian revelation. To have been a witness of it was a distinguishing mark of an apostle (Acts 1: 22). There is no clear heralding of such a doctrine in the Old Testament. The two passages that are thought to come nearest to it are Isa. 26: 19, a passage of difficult interpretation, and Dan. 12: 1, 2, which seems to imply a partial resurrection, and in any case was written well within the period represented by the Apocrypha. The Apocrypha itself does not show a clear anticipation of the Christian conception, but it does show that men were being prepared for such a doctrine. It has to be admitted that much of the Apocrypha echoes the

L

negative attitude of the Old Testament. Ben Sira, for instance, knows of no more future for a man than that of a good name and a son to continue that name. But there are two books that clearly envisage a future life: Wisdom and II Maccabees. The latter book holds out to the martyrs the promise of an everlasting renewal of life (7: 9) and records of one of them that he cherished the hope that God gives of being raised again (7: 14): 'One cannot but choose to die at the hands of men and to cherish the hope that God gives of being raised again by him. But for you there will be no resurrection to life!' The author of the book of Wisdom declares dogmatically that God did not make death (1: 13) and that he 'created man for incorruption, and made him in the image of his own eternity' (2: 23). This latter statement is a re-interpretation of Gen. 1: 26 on a Greek basis, since immortality to the Greek mind was the essence of Godhood. The opening of chapter 3 is a clear statement of the author's conviction that God rewards the righteous with a future life free from torment, 'for though in the sight of men they were punished, their hope is full of immortality' (3: 4). The author of the apocalypse in II Esdras also shows a confident hope in a future life in which the wicked shall suffer and the righteous be vindicated and rewarded in the very presence of God (7: 75–101).

It would be rash to press the claim of intrinsic merit in the Apocrypha too hard in view of the recognized fact that the book is not a unity, and cannot therefore be expected to present a reasoned and detailed account of the events of the period or of the life and thought of the times. There is, indeed, very little recorded of the events of the last two centuries before Christ, except for the story in I and II Maccabees of the struggle for religious freedom. Nor is there any systematic account of the development of doctrine; in fact, each author expresses his own beliefs and reflects his own spiritual background, with the result that we have such disparate views as those of ben Sira, with his two feet firmly placed in the Old Testament thought world, and of the author of the book of Wisdom, who expounds the more up to date views of the Alexandrian, Greek speaking Jews. One might be tempted to say that they cannot both be right, but that would only be true if we could put them in the same setting and let them speak from the same platform and in the same language. But this is just what cannot happen. Moreover, what they said in their own language, the one in Hebrew and the other in Greek, would probably give a somewhat different impression if it were expressed in the other language. Ben Sira's grandson, in fact, was very much aware that even in translation his grandfather's book was likely to differ in sense from what his grandfather intended in Hebrew.

This is one of the factors that has contributed to the intrinsic and abiding worth of the Apocrypha, as indeed of the Old Testament before it, namely, that the writers use their own idiom, write their own thoughts and serve, at least in their conscious effort, their own generation. The picture may be incomplete when the pieces are all put together, but what we do possess is infinitely truer and more trustworthy than if the pieces had been called in by a general editor and made to conform to a common theme. What we have in the Apocrypha is a kind of literary picture gallery hung with paintings of various sizes and merit, but all of them unique and, as they age, becoming more and more valuable and irreplaceable. The effect is comparable with that of a kaleidoscope, offering a different picture at every angle of vision.

The Apocrypha holds its value to the present day and is read by many readers, though doubtless for different reasons. The historian, qua historian, would probably find little to detain him in the stories of Judith and Tobit unless he were seeking information on social and religious background whereas he would feel bound to make the fullest use of I Maccabees and even of II Maccabees, providing he could exercise some control over its facts by reference to other documents. He might also find interest in I Esdras examining afresh the reasons for the publication of a second version of the Biblical book of Ezra (with part of Nehemiah) and attempting to determine the provenance of the story of the three guardsmen and the reason for its inclusion in I Esdras.

A theologian might well concentrate his attention on the books of Ecclesiasticus and Wisdom where he would find different aspects of the Jewish faith set out in strikingly contrasted media, the one in Hebrew and the other in Greek, the one writing as a pastor, the other as a philosopher and man of the world. But other parts of the Apocrypha might well be laid under contribution by him, notably II Maccabees with its emphasis on the intervention of God at every crisis in the course of events.

If the Apocrypha is of importance to both the historian and the theologian as a witness to the life and faith of the period 'between the Testaments', what may the average reader and worshipper expect to find of value and of relevance? Taken at what we may deem its lowest level a man may dip into it and read some of its stories merely for interest, as Pepys seems to have read Tobit on a Sunday afternoon to while away the tedium of a dull sermon. It may be that in reading Tobit for the sake of the story he might become interested in the deep piety of the book and be fired with an enthusiasm for right living and careful and honourable conduct in everyday life. At that point he might find the book of Ecclesiasticus very much to his purpose and might there find the expression of his own hopes and aims. There he will meet a true gentleman in the author, Jesus ben Sira, and within the pages of the book he will be able 'to unearth some of those vivid pictures he conjures up in such deft words of "people we have met"'.[1] He will also find in the author a man of similar passions to himself who, in an 'essay on Things Not To Be Ashamed Of . . . suddenly breaks off for no apparent reason —perhaps his wife interrupted him at this point to tell him of some petty pilfering—into a parenthetical ejaculation: "For an evil wife a seal, and where many hands are a key" xlii. 6'.[2]

If he has a philosophic turn of mind the reader will appreciate the book of Wisdom and will come to feel perhaps that it fills a noticeable gap in the Hebrew canonical literature which has very little reasoned argument within its pages. Not that the book of Wisdom would fully satisfy a quest for religious truth, but it does take a step forward in Jewish thinking by adapting Hebraic ideas to a Greek background of thought and language. In its doctrine of divine wisdom it offers a tentative solution to the problem of how a completely transcendent God can at the same time be at work in the world and among men. Apart from a poem in praise of wisdom in Baruch (3: 9 – 4: 4) the idea of divine wisdom as set out by the author of Wisdom is the last in a series of four such discussions, the earlier ones being Job 28, Proverbs 8, Ecclus. 24. It will be seen at once that two of these are in the Old Testament and two

---

[1] A. D. Power in a preface to his 1939 edition of Ecclesiasticus, p. 14.
[2] A. D. Power, *op. cit.*, p. 12.

in the Apocrypha (three if we count Baruch, but the poem in that book is little more than an echo of things the other writers have said). The conception of divine wisdom first as personified and then as a self-existent entity working on God's behalf among men was one of the most important contributions made towards the problem of how God could be both above the world and in the world, and our knowledge of it would be very limited without the apocryphal material.

But what will the ordinary worshipper find in the Apocrypha when he goes to it expectantly, knowing that for centuries it was held to be included among the scriptures received by the church, even if in a different way from that in which the Old and New Testaments had been received? The answer is that if he goes to it with a faith comparable with that of the men who were its authors he will find expressions of a faith that can match and also strengthen his own faith, he will find examples of lives devoted to the service of God and of courage dedicated to him. He may turn to the book of Judith and find the story of one who was prepared to go to almost any length, save that of submitting her body to a man's lust, in order that her people may be saved from disaster at the hands of the enemy and that they might not have to violate the sacred practices of their religion to save their life. In the book of Tobit the reader will find himself in the atmosphere of a pious Jewish home where great value is set on filial respect and duty and where love of one's neighbour is regarded as the first call upon one's energies. One may wonder a little at the rather harsh austerity of the father in his blindness, but will follow the son with interest as he journeys to recover his father's money and returns home not only with greater wealth than he went out for, but also with a loving wife.

The author's instinct for the true-to-life touch can be seen in the unexpected mention of the dog that went with Tobias and the angel (5: 16): it may be compared with the cattle mentioned at the end of the book of Jonah.

A reader with a love for the heroic will turn to the two books of Maccabees and read there of the Jewish martyrs who suffered for the sake of religious freedom. Particularly poignant are the single-minded zeal of Mattathias and his sons, the nobility of the aged Eleazar who was put to death on the rack after being forced to eat swine's flesh and the courage and selflessness of the mother of seven sons all martyred in her sight. From these he may well turn to the hymn in praise of famous men in Ecclus. 44–50, and note how the author knits together in his praise of God the natural order, the world of nature, which brings its own witness to the wonders of God, and the world of men where God is honoured by the things men do in his name and for his sake.

It will not be long before such a reader will begin to understand why the Apocrypha is, as it were, marginally canonical. It has often contained an authentic word of God for those whose needs are matched by something corresponding to them in one or other of its books or to whose condition it speaks in unmistakable terms if it comes into their hands at the right time. But it is marginal, and there will always be those who 'like Adam Bede, are apt to enjoy "the freedom of occasionally differing from an Apocryphal writer"'.[1]

Mention has been made of the faith in which one may read the books, a faith comparable with that of the men who wrote them. Where faith is exercised there will always be the possibility, the probability indeed, that the spirit of

[1] A. D. Power, *op. cit.*, p. 11.

God will strengthen and confirm all that is done in that faith. It is just this that enables the books of the Apocrypha to hold their place on the margin of the canon, for although the church has been somewhat uncertain in its attitude to them there can be no uncertainty in the mind of the believer for whom the spirit confirms their value. This, indeed, is the attitude of the reformers who believed that scripture 'carried within it its own intrinsic quality',[1] but who also maintained, as set out clearly by Calvin, that the spirit of God confirmed his word: 'Just as God alone is a fitting witness to Himself in His word, so that word will not find the response of faith in the hearts of men before it is sealed by the inner witness of the Spirit'.[2]

[1] H. W. Robinson in his essay 'The Bible as the Word of God' in *The Bible in its Ancient and English Versions*, ed. by H. W. Robinson, 1940, p. 294.

[2] *Institutes*, I. vii. 4.

BIBLIOGRAPHY

A. Bentzen, *Introduction to the Old Testament*, 2 vols., 1948.

F. Buhl, *Canon and Text of the Old Testament*, English trans., 1892.

R. H. Charles (Ed.), *The Apocrypha and Pseudepigrapha of the Old Testament*, 2 vols., 1913.

R. H. Charles, *Religious Development between the Old and the New Testament*. Home University Library, 1914.

J. C. Dancy: *A Commentary on I Maccabees*, 1954.

R. C. Dentan, *The Apocrypha, Bridge of the Testaments*, 1954.

O. Eissfeldt: *Einleitung in das Alte Testament*, 2nd ed. 1956.

F. V. Filson, *Which Books Belong in the Bible?*, 1957.

A. T. S. Goodrick, *The Book of Wisdom*, 1913.

E. J. Goodspeed, *The Story of the Apocrypha*, 1939.

Ch. Guignebert, *The Jewish World in the Time of Jesus*, English trans., 1939.

R. T. Herford, *Talmud and Apocrypha*, 1933.

H. M. Hughes, *The Ethics of Jewish Apocryphal Literature*, (1909?).

M. R. James, *The Book of Tobit and the History of Susanna*, 1929.

C. Lattey, *The Book of Daniel*, 1948 (includes the additions to Daniel).

B. M. Metzger, *An Introduction to the Apocrypha*, 1957.

G. F. Moore, *Judaism in the First Centuries of the Christian Era*, 3 vols., 1927–1930.

W. O. E. Oesterley, *Introduction to the Books of the Apocrypha*, 1935.

W. O. E. Oesterley, *2 Esdras* (Westminster Commentaries), 1933.

C. F. Pfeiffer, *Between the Testaments*, 1959.

R. H. Pfeiffer, *A History of New Testament Times; with an Introduction to the Apocrypha*, 1949.

H. H. Rowley, *The Relevance of Apocalyptic*, 2nd ed. 1947.

D. S. Russell, *Between the Testaments*, 1960.

H. E. Ryle, *The Canon and Text of the Old Testament*, 1892.

C. C. Torrey, *The Apocryphal Literature: a Brief Introduction*, 1945.

G. Wildeboer, *The Origin of the Canon of the Old Testament*, 1895.

H. R. Willoughby, *The Study of the Bible Today and Tomorrow*, 1947. Articles by J. C. Rylaarsdam, 'Intertestamental studies since Charles' Apocrypha and Pseudepigrapha', and R. Marcus, 'The future of intertestamental studies'.

There has been so much literature on the Dead Sea Scrolls that it is not easy to give a select Bibliography. The following six books are suggested as giving a comprehensive survey of the discovery itself, or the literature that was found and of the community that existed there.

T. H. Gaster, *The Scriptures of the Dead Sea Sect*, in English Translation. 1957.

J. T. Milik, *Ten Years of Discovery in the Wilderness of Judaea*, (English Trans. by J. Strugnell) 1959.

Millar Burrows, *The Dead Sea Scrolls*, 1955.

Millar Burrows, *More Light on the Dead Sea Scrolls*, 1958.

Frank Moore Cross, *The Ancient Library of Qumrân*, 1958.

E. F. Sutcliffe, *The Monks of Qumrân*, 1960.

INDEX OF BIBLICAL REFERENCES

Old Testament

Genesis:
1:26 . 64, 129, 156
4:8–13 . . 127
4:10 . . 127
14:1 . . 44
31:47 . 150 n.

Exodus:
3:7 f. . . 127
15 . . 101
23:7 . . 125

Numbers:
15:38 . . 127
20:17 . . 110
21:22 . . 110
22:5, 11 . . 126

Deuteronomy:
8:15 . . 58
13:6 . . 127
28:54 . . 127
29:25–28 . 25 n.
32:10 . . 127

Ruth:
1:16 . . 127

I Kings:
2:3 . . 124
8:38–43 . . 110
9:28 . . 127
10:26 . 45 n.

II Kings:
4:18 ff. . . 48
21:1–18 . . 100

II Chronicles:
33:10–13 . 100
33:18 f. . . 100
35:1–36:21 . 13
35:19 . . 16
35:22 . . 125
36:21 f. . . 124 f.

Ezra:
1:1 . . 124
1:1–11 . . 13
2:1–4:5, 24 . 14
2:63 . 15 n.
3:2 . 25 n.
3:7 . 14 n.
4:7–24 . 13, 17

Ezra:
4:8–6:18; 7:12–26
    18, 150 n.
5:1–10:44 . 14
5:2 . 25 n.

Nehemiah:
7:65 . 15 n.
7:73, 8:1–12 . 14
8:8 . . 16
8:9 . 15 f.
8:13 . 18 n.

Esther:
2:5 . . 53
2:19–23 . . 53
3:1 . . 53
3:13 . . 50
5:1 f. . . 51
8:12 . . 53
9:15, 17 . . 53
9:19 . . 49
9:20–10:3 . 49
9:24 . . 53

Job:
22:14 . . 127
28 . 64, 86

Psalms:
8:4 . . 128
33:1 . . 129
73 . . 63
78 . . 79
79:2 f. . . 110
105 f. . . 79
118 . . 110
136 . . 110
136:1 f. . . 97
148 . . 97

Proverbs:
8 . 60, 64, 78
8:30 . . 65
11:21 . . 125

Ecclesiastes:
12:7 . . 62

Isaiah:
3:10 . . 58
5:22 . . 127
5:24 . . 128
24–27 . . 7
24:8 . . 128
26:19 . 63, 155

Isaiah:
28:1, 2 . . 127
28:15, 18 . . 63
29:16 . . 61
40 ff. . . 80
40:15 . . 58
42:8 . . 127
44:9–20 . . 91
44:20 . . 58
59:17 . . 61
61:10 . . 127

Jeremiah:
10:1–16 . . 92
10:11 . 150 n.
18:18 . . 75
22:24 . . 127
25:9–12 . . 13
26:17–19 . 124
29 . . 91
29:10 . . 13
43:6, 7 . . 87

Lamentations:
3:44 . . 128
5:11, 13 . . 128

Ezekiel:
1:1 . 26 f.
28:3 . . 97
38, 39 . . 7

Daniel:
2:4–7:28 . 150 n.
2:22 f. . . 18
2:37 . . 18
3:8 . . 69
3:23 f. . . 96
3:25, 28 . . 153
4:13, 17, 23, 31 153
5:2 . . 87
6:22 . . 153
7:3 . 24 n.
7:10 . . 153
8:15 f. . . 153
9:2 . . 124
9:4–19 . 86, 88
10:13 . . 153
11 . . 4
11:31 . 110, 127
12 . . 96
12:1, 2 . . 155
12:2 . . 63
12:11 . . 110

Hosea:
4:7 . . 126
11:1 . . 83

Joel:
2:17 . . 126

Amos
3:1–8 . 22 n.

Obadiah:
18 . . 128

Zechariah:
9–14 . . 7

Apocrypha

I Esdras:
1:23 f. . . 16
1:28 . . 125
1:57 f.; 2:1 . 125
2:1–11 . . 16
2:12 . 14 n.
2:16–30 . . 17
4:10a . . 18
4:13 . . 15
4:29 . 17 n.
4:43–46 . 14 n., 16
4:57–61 . 14 n.
4:59, 60 . . 18
5:1–6 . . 16
5:49 . . 126
7:6, 9 . . 126
9:48 . . 16
9:49 . 15 f.

II Esdras:
3:1 . . 27
7:28 . . 26
7:36–105 . 28 n.
7:75–101 . 156
8:34 . . 128
8:45 . . 126
10:22 . . 128
11:37 . 27 n.
14:44–47 . 134
1:21 f. . . 37
3:8 . . 153
5:16 . . 161
5:16, 21 . . 153
6:7 . . 153
7:13 . . 126
8:3 . . 153
8:15 . . 153
11:14 . . 153
11:18 . 38 n.
12:15 . . 153
14:10 . 37, 38 n.

Judith:
1:1 . . 44

Judith:
1:6 . . 44
1:14 . . 126
2:4 . . 44
2:7 . . 126
3:8 . . 47
4:3 . . 44
4:6 . . 44
4:13 . . 127
5:5 ff. . . 48
5:17 ff. . . 47
6:2 . 47, 127
7:18 . . 126
8:3 . . 48
8:5, 6 . . 46
9:2–14 . . 46
11:10 . . 46
11:13, 14 . 46
11:17 . . 46
11:23 . . 127
12:2, 8, 9 . 46
12:6 . . 46
12:11 . . 44
13:4, 7 . . 46
14:10 . . 47
15:1–7 . . 48
16:2–17 . 47 f.
16:18, 19 . 47

Additions to Esther:
11:1 . . 136
11:2–4 . . 53
12:1–6 . . 53
12:6 . . 53
13:6 . . 53
16:10 . . 53

Wisdom:
1:1 . . 69
1:13 . 64, 156
1:16 . . 63
2:1–20 . . 58
2:3 . . 63
2:12 . 58, 128
2:23 . 64, 129, 156
3:1 . . 64
3:4 . . 156
3:7 . . 128
3:16 . . 69
4:6 . . 69
4:12 . 59 n.
4:20 . . 63
5:18–20 . . 61
6:1–3, 9 . . 69
6:17–20 . . 59
7:1 ff. . 67, 86
7:22 ff. . . 59
7:24, 27 . 154
7:27 . . 154

Wisdom:
8:7 . . 59
8:19 . . 151
8:19 f. . . 62
9:8 . . 67
9:15 . 59, 62
9:17 . . 67
10–19 . . 61
10, 11 . . 79
10:3 . . 127
10:17 . . 70
11:4 . 55, 128
11:5 . . 56
11:16 . 56, 63
11:17 . 60, 129
11:22 . 58, 128
11:26 . 59 n.
12–14 . . 61
12:12 . . 61
12:19 . . 69
14:21 . . 127
14:25 ff. . . 61
15:8 . . 62
15:10 . 58, 128
16:25 . 59 n.
17:12 . . 60

Ecclesiasticus:
1:10 . . 82
1:14 . . 78
1:26 . . 78
2:1–6 . . 83
2:7–11 . . 83
2:10 . . 147
3:17–24 . . 83
4:1–10 . . 83
5:6 . . 83
6:20–31 . . 74
6:30 . . 127
6:37 . . 79
7:18 . . 127
9:1 . . 127
9:12 . . 125
15:9 . . 129
16:24 f. . . 72
17:3 . . 129
17:22 . . 127
18:13, 14 . 82
23:1 . . 82
24 . 66, 78, 86
24:3 . . 78
24:5 . . 127
24:8, 23 . . 83
24:23 . 79, 154
24:30–32 . . 77
25:24 . . 84
31:25 . . 127
34:11 f. . . 76

Ecclesiasticus:
35:17 . .	128
35:18–20 .	72
36:1–17 .	72
38, 39 .	75
39:1	80, 130 n.
39:4 .	76
39:15–40:7 .	74
41:1, 2 .	84
41:3, 4 .	84
42:6 .	159
42:9–14 .	84
44–49 .	80
44:3–5 .	80
44:8, 13 .	84
45:23 .	76
45:24 f. .	81
46:1 .	83
46:11, 12 .	130
47:1 .	81
48:22 .	81
48:24 .	80
49:4 .	76
49:8, 9 .	80 n.
49:10 .	80
49:13 .	15 n.
49:15 .	81
50:1–4 .	75
50:27 .	75
51:23, 25 .	77

Baruch:
1:1–9 .	86
1:1, 3, 14 .	87
1:2 .	88
1:10–14 .	87
1:10–3:8 .	87
1:20 .	127
1:20 f. .	125
2:2 .	126
2:3, 24 .	88
2:8–19 .	86, 88
2:17 .	88
2:26 .	88
2:28 .	125
3:9–4:4	86 f., 159
4:1	79 n., 154
4:5–5:9 .	87
4:25 .	87
4:31–34 .	87
5:2 .	127
5:5–9 .	86

Prayer of Azariah and
Song of the Three
Young Men:
15 .	96
35–65 .	97
67 f. .	97

Susanna:
3 . .	126
54 f., 58 f. .	98
62 .	126

1 Maccabees:
1:9, 12 .	111
1:24–28 .	107
1:36–40 .	107
1:54	102 n., 110, 127
1:56 f. .	109
2:7–13 .	107
2:41 .	106, 116
2:42 .	106
2:49 ff. .	106
2:51–68 .	79
2:52–60 .	110
3:3–9 .	107
3:45 .	107, 110
4:24 .	110
4:30–33 .	110
4:46 .	109, 131
4:47, 53 .	126
4:56 ff. .	112 n.
5:10–13 .	109
5:48 .	110
5:62 .	106
6:34 .	111 n.
6:39 .	107
7:17 .	110
7:33 .	107
7:37 .	110
8:17 .	123
8:17–32 .	120
8:23–32 .	109
9:27 .	109, 131
9:39 .	107
9:43 ff. .	106
9:54 .	109
10:18–20, 25–45	109
11:30–37 .	108 f.
12:6–18, 20–23	109
13:3 .	106
13:42 .	106
14:4–15 .	107
14:6–15 .	110
14:18, 27 .	108
14:20–23 .	109
14:25 .	106
14:27–45 .	109
14:28 .	111
14:41 .	109, 131
14:48 f. .	108
15:2–9, 16–21	109
16:2 .	106
16:24 .	109

II Maccabees:
1:7 .	122 n.

II Maccabees:
1:9 .	112 n.
1:10–2:18	122 n.
1:11–18 .	118
1:29 .	126
2:2 .	92
2:19–22 .	117
2:23 .	122 f.
2:23–32 .	120
3:22–30 .	115
4:1–6 .	116
4:11 .	120
4:17 .	116
4:38 .	116 n.
5:1–4 .	115
5:6, 10 .	116 n.
5:17–20 .	119
6:11 .	116
6:12 .	116
7:1–20 .	106
7:6 .	126
7:9 .	156
7:9, 14, 23, 36	116
7:14 .	156
8:3 .	127
8:23, 36 .	116 n.
8:25 ff. .	116
9:5 .	116 n.
9:12 .	119
10:1–8 .	117
10:3 .	118, 120
10:6 .	117
10:6 f. .	112 n.
10:29–31 .	115
11:6 .	153
11:8 .	115
11:13 .	116 n.
12:38 .	116
12:40 .	119, 126
12:43 .	116
12:43–45 .	116 n.
13:8 .	116 n.
13:19–26 .	121
14:37–46 .	119
15:1 f. .	116
15:6–19 .	119
15:12–16 .	115
15:23 .	153
15:26, 27 .	115
15:36 .	117

New Testament

Luke:
24:44 .	133

Acts:
1:22 .	155

Romans:
1:18–32 . . 61
5:3–5 . . 59
8:30 . . 59
9:19, 20 . . 61
9:19–23 . . 61

Ephesians:
6:11–17 . . 61

II Timothy:
3:16 . . 126

Hebrews:
11 . . 79

Revelation:
5:5   24 n., 27 n.
14:8 . . 27
16:19 . . 27
17:5 . . 27
18:10 . . 27

GENERAL INDEX

AARON, 76, 80 f.
Abomination of desolation, 110.
Abraham, 110
Achiacharus, *see* Ahikar
Achior, 41 f., 47 f.
Adam as the first sinner, 30
Africanus, 139
Ahasuerus, 53
Ahikar (Achiacharus), 33, 36 ff.
Ahura Mazda, 65
Alcimus, 103 f.
Aldine Greek Bible, 142
Alexander Balas, 104
Alexander Jannaeus, 8, 45
Alexander the Great, 3, 56
Alexandra, 8
Alexandria, 10, 21 n., 56 f., 69 f., 122 f., 136, 150, 157
Alexandrian Canon, 138
Ambrose of Milan, 23
Ammonites, 41, 103
Angels, 152 f.
Anna, 33 ff.
Antiochus III, the Great, 75
Antiochus IV, Epiphanes, 4 f., 9, 43, 45, 77, 102 f., 113 ff.
Antiochus V, Eupator, 103, 117
Antiochus VI, 104 n., 105 f.
Antiochus VII, Sidetes, 105
Apame, 17 n.
Apocalypse of Baruch, 11
Apocalyptic, 7, 20, 25 ff. 89, 151

Apocrypha, meaning of, 132
Arabians, 21
Archangels, 30
Arioch, 44
Aristobulus II, 8
Arphaxad, 40, 44
Artabazos III, 17 n.
Artaxerxes I, 13, 17
Artaxerxes (? = Xerxes), 50, 53
Artaxerxes III, Ochus, 44
Arzareth, 25
Asa, 81
Asaramel, 111
Asmodeus, 33 f., 36 n., 153
Assumption of Moses, 11
Athanasius, 138
Attharates, 15
Augustine, 139
Augustus, 24 n.
Aurelian, 22 n.
Authorized Version, 145
Azariah, Prayer of, 93, 96 f.

Babylon, 36, 88 ff.
Bacchides, 103 f.
Baenites, 103
Bagoas, 44
Bar Cochbar revolt, 31
Baruch, Book of, 11, 85 ff., 92, 138, 140, 143
II Baruch and II Esdras, 29 ff.
Bel and the Dragon, 93 ff.
Belshazzar, 85, 87 f.
Ben Sira, 66, 71 ff., 110, 129 ff., 156 f., 159
Benedicite, the, 97
Benedictus, the, 101
Bethulia, 40 f.

Bible Society, the, 147
Bodenstein, Andreas, *see* Karlstadt
Bunyan, John, 146

Canon of Scripture, 2 f., 12, 80, 109 f., 125, 133, 136
Calvin, 162
Canaanites, 68
Canticles, *see* Song of Songs
Carmonians, 21
Cartwright, 145
Cendebaus, 105
Chanukka, festival of, 117
Chronicler, the, 15 ff., 81 f., 100, 114, 124
Chronicles, Books of, 101
Codex, books in form of, 136
Council of Trent, 141
Coverdale, 142 f.
Cranmer, 143
Cromwell, Thomas, 143
Cyprian, 71
Cyrus, 14 n., 16

Daniel, 81, 97, 110
Daniel, Additions to, 93 ff., 100
Daniel, Book of, 7, 81 f., 95 f., 110, 124, 152
Darius, 13, 16 f.
David, 76, 81, 101, 110
Dead Sea Discoveries, 8 f.
Dead Sea Scrolls, 11, 130; *see also* Qumrân
Deborah, 47, 83
Demetrius I, 103
Demetrius II, 104 f.
Desecration of Temple, 117, 119

Deutero-canonical
books, 133
Deutero-Isaiah, 91 f.
Didascalia, 101
Dispersion of the Jews,
37, 135, 150
Domitian, 24 n., 27

Ecclesiastes, 3, 56, 58 f.,
82, 135
Ecclesiasticus, 9, 56,
60, 69, 71 ff., 134,
140 f., 143
Ecclesiasticus, Prologue
to, 11, 19 n., 133, 135
Edomites, 103
Egypt, 37, 55, 69, 75,
87, 112, 122
Egyptians, 68 f.
Eleazar, the Maccabee,
103, 113
Eleazar, the Martyr,
113, 123
Elephantine, Aramaic
papyri from, 37
I Enoch, 10, 134
II Enoch, 11
Epicureans, 54, 58
Esarhaddon, 33, 37
I Esdras, 10, 13 ff.,
140 ff.
II Esdras, 7, 11, 20 ff.,
140 ff.
Essenes, 8 f.
Esther, 83
Esther, Book of, 7, 82,
117, 135 f., 138
Esther, additions to, 10,
49 ff., 100
Euergetes, 75
Exile, 13, 35 f., 85, 87, 130
Exodus, the, 55, 69
Exodus, Book of, 129 f.
Ezekiel, Book of, 135
Ezra, 14 f., 20 ff., 76, 82

Gabael, 34
Gabriel, 153
Gallienus, 21 n.
Geneva Bible, 144
Greek, in the Book of
Wisdom, 59
Greek thought and He-
brew thought, 61 ff.,
150
Gregory of Nyssa, 132
Guardsmen, story of the
three, 13 ff.

Habakkuk, 98
Haman, 50, 53
Hasideans, 102 f.
Hasmoneans, 8, 105 f.,
110
Heavenly visions, 115,
119
Hebrew and Greek
thought, 61 ff., 150
Hellenism, 5, 43, 56 f.
Hellenization of Judaea,
4 f., 113
Herod the Great, 1, 8
Hezekiah, 76, 81 f., 101
Holofernes, 40 ff.
Hyrcanus, John, 6, 8, 45,
49, 105 f., 109
Hyrcanus II, 8

Idolatry, 55, 61, 90 ff.,
119
Image worship, 70 n.
Immortality, 54, 59,
63 f., 69, 156
Isaiah, 81
Isaiah, Book of, 130

Jael, 47, 83
Jamnia, Jewish scholars
at, 2, 135
Jason, 5, 113
Jason of Cyrene, 10,
112, 118, 120, 122 f.
Jeconiah, 85
Jehoiakim, 85
Jehoshaphat, 81
Jeremiah, 87, 90 f., 112,
124
Jeremiah, Book of, 92
Jeremiah, Letter of, 1 f.,
90 ff., 134, 138
Jeremiel, 30
Jerome, 68, 132, 138 f.
Jerusalem, fall of in
586 B.C., 34 f., 85, 87,
92
Jerusalem, fall of in
70 A.D., 10, 12, 25, 27,
31
Jewish revolt of A.D.
66–70, 1, 10, 88
Joakim, 40, 44
Job, Book of, 56, 60
Joel, Book of, 7
John, father of Eupole-
mus, 120
John Hyrcanus, *see*
Hyrcanus

Jonah, 35, 101
Jonathan Maccabeus,
6, 104, 110
Joseph, 81
Josephus, 2 n., 3 n., 6 n.,
11, 18, 52, 75, 97,
105 ff., 133
Joshua, 83
Josiah, 14, 76, 81
Jubilees, Book of, 7, 134
Judas Maccabeus, 102 f.,
113, 115 ff.
Judges, Book of, 130
Judith, 41 ff.
Judith, Book of, 6, 40 ff.,
138, 140 f.

Karlstadt, 132, 140
Kerman, 21 n.

Lamentations, Book of,
82, 92, 138
Law, 109, 124
Law, identified with
Wisdom, 66, 79
Letter of Jeremiah, 1 f.,
90 ff., 134, 138
Life of Adam and Eve,
11
Luther, 35, 140
Lysias, 103, 114

Maccabean revolt, 4 ff.,
36, 43, 45, 77, 105,
118 f.
I Maccabees, 9, 102 ff.
II Maccabees, 10, 112 ff.,
153
I and II Maccabees, 7,
140
III Maccabees, 123
IV Maccabees, 123
Man, idea of in Wisdom,
62 f.
Manasseh, Prayer of,
100 f., 140 f., 143
Martin Marprelate, *see*
Penry
Martyrdom, stories of,
119
Mattathias, 102, 106
Matthew's Bible, 143 f.
Melito, 138
Menelaus, 5, 113
Messianic Age, 23, 26
Mica(ia)h, 124
Michael, 153
Minor Prophets, 80

Mordecai, 50 f.
Moses, 80
Muratorian Fragment, 68

Nabunaid, 88
Nabateans, 104
Nadab, 38
Nathan, 81
Nebuchadnezzar, 40 f., 44 f., 47, 85, 87 f.
Nehemiah, 15, 76, 82, 112, 122
Nero, 69
Nicanor, 103, 113, 115, 120
Nicanor's day, 117

Odenathus, 22 n.
Odes, the, 97, 101
Old Testament, in Apocrypha, 124 ff.
Olivetan, 143
Oniads and Tobiads, 5, 116
Onias, 5, 113
Origen, 111, 138 f.
Osiander, Andreas, 142

Palestinian Canon, 138
Paul, 61
Penry, John, 145
Pepys, Samuel, 147
Pharisees, 8, 45 f., 76, 106, 116
Philistines, 110
Philo, 11, 68, 70, 133
Plato, 59, 129
Pompey, 1, 8, 88, 110
Prophecy, cessation of, 109, 130 f.
Prophetic writings, canon of, 124
Proverbs, Book of, 56, 60, 129
Psalms, Book of, 129
Psalms of Solomon, 10
Pseudepigrapha, 133
Pseudonymity, 27, 55, 67 f., 89, 91, 152
Ptolemaic rule, 3
Ptolemy Lagos, 17 n.
Ptolemy IV Philopator, 123

Ptolemy VI, 104
Ptolemy XII, 52
Purification, festival of, 117, 120
Purim, 49, 51

Queen of Heaven, worship of, 65
Qumrân, texts from, 8 f., 35 n., 74, 98, 108, 134

Rahab, 83
Raguel, 33 f.
Ramiel, 30
Raphael, 33 f., 37, 39, 153
Raphia, battle of, 123
Resurrection, 155 f.
Return from Exile, 13, 15, 44
Revelation, Book of, 132
Rome, 24 n., 27 f., 88 f., 104 f., 123
Rufinus, 139
Ruth, Book of, 82

Sabbath observance, 106
Sadducees, 76, 106, 116
Salathiel, 23, 25, 28 f.
Samaritan Pentateuch, 80
Samuel, 81
Sapor I, 22 n., 23
Sarah, 33 f., 39
Sarbeth Sabanaiel, 111
Saul, 81
Scripture, 126; *see also* Canon
Sennacherib, 33
Septuagint, the, 17, 57 f., 95, 98, 127, 136
Shalmanezer, 25, 33, 36
Shealtiel, 25
Sheshbazzar, 14 n.
Sibylline Oracles, 10
Seleucus Nicator, 17 n.
Simon Maccabeus, 6, 9, 102 f., 105, 108 f.
Simon the Just, 3, 6, 75 f.
Sisera, 47

Solomon, 55, 59, 67, 81
Song of Songs, 3, 82, 135
Sorites, 59
Spirit of God, 78
Spitamenes, 17 n.
Susanna, 93 f., 96 ff., 125

Temple, desecration of, 117, 119
Temple, festival of rededication, 117
Testament of the Twelve Patriarchs, 134
Theodotion, 95, 97
Tiamat, 98
Tiberius Alexander, 69
Tirshatha, 15
Titus, 24 n., 27, 88
Tobiads, 116
Tobias, 33 ff.
Tobit, Book of, 4, 9, 33 ff., 134, 138, 140 f., 147, 152 f.
Trypho, 104 f.

Uriel, 30
Uzziah, 41 f.

Valerian, 22 n.
Vespasian, 11, 24 n., 27, 88
Vulgate, 71, 92, 138, 141

Westminster Confession, 146
Whitgift, 145
Wisdom, Book of, 10, 54 ff., 138, 140 f, 157
Wisdom, conception of divine, 55 ff., 60, 64 ff., 78 f., 85, 153 ff.
Word of God, 78
Writings, the, 82

Xerxes I, 53

Zealots, 8 f.
Zenobia, 22 n.
Zerubbabel, 13 ff., 25, 29
Zürich Bible, 142